Tales from the Cubs Dugout

Pete Cava

Sports Publishing, L.L.C.
www.SportsPublishingLLC.com

Director of Production: Susan M. Moyer
Project manager: Jay Peterson
Dustjacket design: Christina Cary

Dustjacket photo courtesy of the *Chicago Sun-Times,* Inc.

ISBN: 1-58261-497-0

Printed in the United States of America.

SPORTS PUBLISHING, L.L.C.
804 NORTH NEIL STREET
CHAMPAIGN, ILLINOIS 61820
www.SportsPublishingLLC.com

For my wife, Molly Mehagan Cava,
born four days after her beloved Cubs played their
last World Series game to date.

ACKNOWLEDGMENTS

The author gratefully acknowledges the contributions and cooperation of Hal Bateman, Dr. Peter Bjarkman, Ollan Cassell, Dick Cassin, Andy Cava, Molly Cava, Nancy Cava, Paul Debono, Dick Denny, Reid Duffy, Jim Fishman, Kurt Freudenthal, Charlie Holdaway, Steve Holdaway, Margaret Mavor, Glen McMicken, Mark Murrow, Dan O'Brien, Anne Phillips, Dale Ratermann, Tom Surber, and the late Harold Rosenthal, as well as the Society for American Baseball Research, the sports department of *The Indianapolis Star,* the Indiana State Library, Indianapolis/Marion County Library, Butler University's Irwin Library, and the Ziffren Sports Resource Center Library of the Amateur Athletic Foundation of Los Angeles.

CONTENTS

Grover Alexander

Grover Alexander won 373 games between 1911 and 1930 and was elected to the Hall of Fame in 1937. He was with the Phillies from 1911 to 1917, the Cubs from 1918 through 1926 and the Cardinals from 1926 through 1929.

The right-hander's greatest years were with Philadelphia, and his most unforgettable performance took place when he pitched for St. Louis during the 1926 World Series.

Yet Alexander the Great pitched more games for the Cubs than for any other team.

When Alexander was a boy, a younger brother had trouble pronouncing his name and called him "Doder". The nickname stuck, and gradually evolved into "Dode". That's what folks called Alexander back in his hometown of St. Paul, Nebraska.

In the big leagues, however, Grover was known as "Alex", "Ol' Pete", or "Alexander the Great".

Alexander was named for Grover Cleveland, the President of the United States from 1885 to 1889 and from 1893 to 1897.

In *The Winning Team,* a 1952 film about Alexander's life, a former Cubs radio broadcaster named Dutch Reagan played the role of Ol' Pete. Dutch, better known as Ronald Wilson Reagan, would later become President of the United States in 1981 . . . making Ol' Pete Alexander the only athlete portrayed on-screen by a future U.S. President.

Although he'd averaged over 30 wins a season for the Phillies from 1914 through 1917, Philadelphia owner William Baker traded Alexander to the Cubs prior to the 1918 season. The United States was at war with Germany, and Baker was concerned about the possibility of losing Alexander to military service.

Baker traded Alexander and catcher Bill Killefer for Pickles Dillhoefer, another backstop, pitcher Mike Prendergast, and cash. Baker was also concerned about Alexander's age since, by then, Ol' Pete was 30 years old.

The trade was one of the biggest steals in Cubs history. Prendergast, 9-17 in two seasons with the Cubs, won 13 of 28 decisions in a couple of years at Philadelphia.

With the Cubs from 1918 through June 1926, Alexander won 128 games against 83 defeats, including a 27-14 log in 1920 with a league-leading 173 strikeouts.

Alexander was the Cubs' Opening Day pitcher for 1918, but pitched just twice more before he was drafted into the army. Ol' Pete served in France as a frontline sergeant in the artillery.

He returned home deaf in one ear. Worse, he had developed epilepsy and was drinking heavily.

After the war, Alexander's favorite drinking partner in Chicago was "Shufflin' Phil" Douglas, a lanky Southerner. When sober, Douglas could be a topnotch pitcher. By July 1919, he'd won ten games for the Cubs against six losses.

Hoping to keep his star pitcher out of the saloons, club president William Veeck (whose son, Bill Veeck, later owned the White Sox), decided it was time to separate Alexander and Douglas. On July 25, 1919, just two days after the hard-drinking teammates had thrown back-to-back shutouts in a double header with Brooklyn, Veeck traded Douglas to the New York Giants.

The deal didn't help, as Alexander lapsed deeper into the bottle.

Douglas was barred from baseball for life after confiding to a Cardinals player he would leave the Giants in the middle of the 1922 pennant race in return for "an inducement".

Teammates remembered Alexander as a big guy with a fine build who liked chewing tobacco. He wore his baseball cap one size too small, and tugged it down rakishly to one side. Unlike most of the other pitchers of his era, Alexander managed to stay in shape without running between starts.

Alexander had short fingers and threw a heavy ball. Hans Lobert, a big league catcher from 1903 to 1917, got hit above the heart by an Alexander fastball. Lobert said it "bore in like a lump of lead . . . I couldn't get my breath for 10 minutes afterward."

S everal times a season, Alexander would suffer an epileptic seizure on the bench. As teammates tried to keep the luckless pitcher from swallowing his tongue, Alexander would thrash around and froth at the mouth.

Once the players had Alexander pinned to the ground, one of them would pour a shot of brandy down his throat in the belief the spirits would revive him. Alexander's teammates usually kept a bottle on hand in the event of an emergency.

Amazingly, Alexander never suffered a seizure while he was on the mound. Sometimes he sipped ammonia on the bench, hoping to ward off attacks.

A lexander's 300th career win came in a Cubs uniform on September 20, 1924. His Opening Day win on April 14, 1925, the first Cubs game ever aired on radio, was his 301st.

Alexander helped his own cause in the 8-2 win over the Pirates, homering his first time up. He also had a double and a single.

Alcoholism eventually led to Alexander's departure from Chicago. By 1926 Joe McCarthy was managing the Cubs. Marse Joe believed Ol' Pete was a bad influence on the younger players.

"A fellow once asked me one time if Alex followed the rules," said McCarthy. "'Sure he did,' I said. 'But they were always Alex's rules.' So I had to let him go."

McCarthy also had his hands full with another carouser, outfielder Hack Wilson. While Wilson was only 26 and just coming into his own as a slugger, Alexander was a shopworn 39-year-old.

In mid-June McCarthy unloaded the veteran pitcher to St. Louis for the $4,000 waiver price.

Ol' Pete made history that fall in the World Series. After winning two starts against the mighty Yankees, Alexander came on in relief with the bases loaded in the seventh inning of the seventh game. He struck out Tony Lazzeri, a dangerous batter, and went on to preserve a 3-2 Cardinals victory.

Some teammates claimed Alexander had been out on the town the night before the game, and was still feeling the effects when he came in to face Lazzeri.

Despite the ravages of combat, drink, and illness, Alexander was one of the greatest pitchers of all time. He could throw a fastball, curve, screwball, sinker, and change-up.

Unfortunately, Ol' Pete was his own worst enemy.
"I had control of everything," he lamented, "but myself."

Bob Anderson and the Two-Balls-in-Play Incident

A strapping, blond right-hander from Hammond, Indiana, Bob Anderson pitched for the Cubs from 1957 through 1962. He was supposed to be the Cubs' starter for the opening day game with the Los Angeles Dodgers in 1959, but a spring blizzard hit Chicago and the contest was postponed.

Before the game was canceled, however, the 6'4", 210-pound Anderson came ambling out of the Cubs' dugout bundled up in his bright blue warm-up jacket and a pair of winter gloves. He sculpted a melon-sized snowball and, to the delight of newspaper wire services photographers, cheerfully tossed it around with batterymate Sammy Taylor.

A nderson pitched for the 1956 Los Angeles Angels, one of the best teams in Pacific Coast League history. The Angels

went 107-56 that year, with Anderson winning 12 of 16 decisions. The pitching staff also included future Cubbies Dave Hillman (21-7), Gene Fodge (19-7), Dick Drott, and Johnny Briggs (5-5).

After his fine work with the Los Angeles squad, Bob Scheffing took over as Chicago's skipper. Scheffing and pitching coach Fred Fitzsimmons pinned their hopes on the new kids, as well as a young right-hander out of Trinity College in Connecticut named Moe Drabowsky.

With the Cubs, however, Anderson, Hillman, Fodge, Drott, Briggs, and Drabowsky would combine for just 113 wins against 159 losses.

Anderson holds a unique niche in baseball lore. Of the hundreds of big league hurlers from Don Aase to George Zuverink, he's the only one ever to be on the mound while more than one baseball was in play.

This bizarre incident took place during a Cubs-Cardinals game on June 30, 1959. With one out in the fourth inning, Stan Musial came to the plate. Stan the Man worked the count to 3-and-1, and Anderson threw him a high, inside fastball.

Musial turned into the pitch, then seemed to hold up. The ball jumped, nicked home plate umpire Vic Delmore's shoulder, and traveled all the way to the backstop. Delmore called ball four and motioned Musial toward first base. Catcher Sammy Taylor spun around to argue, claiming the ball had ticked Musial's bat before it grazed Delmore.

While Taylor stood with his back to the field, Anderson strolled toward home plate as Musial sauntered to first. Cubs manager Bob Scheffing rumbled out of the dugout to add his voice to the protest. No one, however, asked for time.

The ump, seeing Anderson coming toward him with upraised palms, assumed the hurler wanted a new baseball. As Delmore tossed one to Anderson, Cubs' third baseman Alvin Dark alertly scampered toward the backstop for the original ball.

Musial, hoping to take advantage of the confusion, rounded first base and took off for second. At about that time, Dark reached the backstop, where Cubs' on-field announcer Pat Pieper had grabbed the original baseball and had dropped it into a ball bag.

Meanhile, Anderson spotted Musial's dash and whirled and fired toward second base. As Anderson threw, another baseball whizzed over his head toward second. Musial slid as Anderson's toss sailed into center field. Musial scrambled to his feet with an eye on third base. As he stepped off the bag, he was tagged out by Chicago shortstop Ernie Banks.

Dark had retrieved a ball from Pieper, and he and Anderson had simultaneously thrown toward second. While a stunned Musial tried to figure out what was going on, both dugouts emptied. Scheffing and St. Louis manager Solly Hemus engaged in a three-way shouting match with Delmore and fellow umps Al Barlick, Bill Jackowski, and Shag Crawford.

The umpires finally decided that the first baseball—the one thrown by Dark—was indeed the ball in play, and the one thrown by Anderson was a dead ball. Musial, they declared, was out at second. Enraged, the Cardinals announced the game was under protest. They dropped it, however, after posting a 4-1 victory.

Anderson finished the '59 season year with a 12-13 record and was 9-11 in 1960. After that, arm trouble diminished his fast ball. He spent most of 1961 and 1962 in the Cubs bullpen, and was traded to Detroit. He bowed out of the major leagues following a 3-1 record with a 3.30 earned run average for the Tigers in '63.

A graduate of Western Michigan University, Anderson retired from Inland Steel in 1993. He still gets frequent requests for details of the two-balls-in-play incident from over four decades ago.

Cap Anson

The history of the Cubs dates back to 1871, when a franchise called the Chicago White Stockings played in the National Association of Professional Baseball Players, commonly called the National Association.

After sputtering in and out of the professional ranks, the White Stockings joined the fledgling National League and played their first game on April 25, 1876—exactly two months before Custer and the Seventh Cavalry met their fate at Little Big Horn.

One of the original White Stockings was third baseman Adrian "Cap" Anson, baseball's first superstar.

Anson was a five-year National Association veteran who had played for Rockford, Illinois, and the Philadelphia Athletics. Al Spalding signed him to a contract with Chicago for 1876, but the Athletics offered Anson $500 more than Chicago was paying to tear up the contract and return to Philadelphia.

Anson's fiancee was a Philadelphian and didn't want to leave her hometown. She begged Anson to accept the offer from

the Athletics and renege on the deal with Chicago. Anson asked Spalding to tear up the Chicago contract, but Spalding insisted that Anson stick by the terms of the agreement.

Anson took the unprecedented step of offering to buy out his own contract for $1,000 . . . but Spalding—who was building a championship team—wouldn't budge. Anson finally gave in. So did Anson's fiancee, who reluctantly agreed to leave Philadelphia.

It was a recalcitrant Anson who joined his Chicago teammates in the spring of 1876.

On his first day with his new club, Anson showed up in street clothes. He couldn't resist tossing the ball around with his new teammates. When Spalding saw Anson in mufti, playing catch with the other Chicago players, he issued an order.

"Now Anse," Spalding informed his prize recruit, "come tomorrow in uniform."

Anson would stay in a Chicago uniform for the next 22 seasons.

Anson helped the White Stockings to the 1876 N.L. title and, after taking over as manager and shifting to first base in 1879, he led the club to pennants in 1880, 1881, 1882, 1885, and 1886.

The White Stockings were also known as Anson's Colts and, after Cap's departure, they were dubbed the Orphans.

The March 27, 1902, edition of the *Chicago Daily News* referred to Chicago's youthful newcomers as "Cubs." Several years later, that became the team's official nickname.

The first player to accumulate 3,000 career hits, Anson batted over .300 in all but two of his 22 N.L. seasons. He was the first batter to hit three consecutive home runs in a game. Anson was an innovator who insisted on training rules for his players and a formalized spring training regimen.

His teams were among the first to employ base stealing and hit-and-run plays on a regular basis, and Anson was the first manager to experiment with a pitching rotation. He took part in a baseball tour of England in 1874 and a global junket in 1888-1889. In 1939 Anson—who was once elected city clerk of Chicago—was voted into baseball's Hall of Fame.

Anson was still an everyday player when he turned 40 in 1892. Sportswriters had begun calling him "Pop" and "Old Man." Some suggested Anson should hang up his spikes and make room for a younger player. The jibes began to irritate Anson, who felt he was still one of the league's top players.

The Chicago captain decided on a satirical revenge. He trotted out to his position one day sporting a shaggy, gray wig and a long, gray fake beard. Anson played the entire contest wearing the wig and beard. Even the reporters had to chuckle.

Anson, noted a sympathetic scribe, "undertook to revenge himself on his critics in a manner every way worthy of his great intellect . . . it was daring; it was original and conspicuous and particularly humorous . . ."

The burly 6', 200-pound Iowa native played before fielder's gloves came into fashion and, for much of his career, the pitcher's mound was 45' or 50' from home plate, instead of the present 60' 6" distance. He was a strict disciplinarian who wouldn't hesitate to back his words with his fists.

Although a college man—he helped form Notre Dame's first baseball team while attending school there in 1869—the light-haired, ruddy-complected Anson was a vicious bench jockey and a well-known umpire-baiter. If Anson didn't like an umpire's decision, he would launch into a profanity-laced tirade.

Anson was generally despised throughout the league, but Chicago fans loved him.

Although honest and religious, Anson was also an unapolo-getic bigot. He frequently told ethnic jokes about the Irish, Jews, and blacks and openly used racial slurs.

In July 1887 the White Stockings scheduled an exhibition game with Newark of the International League. Newark's starting pitcher was to be a black man named George Stovey.

While African American players were rare in the 19th Century, there was no institutionalized color barrier. Two blacks had played for Toledo's major league team in the American Association, and over thirty more had competed at the minor league level.

Anson insisted the White Stockings wouldn't take the field against a team with a black player in the line-up. Backing down to Anson, who was one of the most influential men in baseball, the Newark club benched Stovey.

A nson's attitude toward African Americans was never fully explained and completely unjustified.

"His repugnant feeling . . . toward colored ball players," observed Negro League player and historian Sol White, ". . . and his opposition, with his great popularity and power in baseball circles, hastened the exclusion of the black man from the white leagues."

Part of Anson's legacy was the segregation of professional baseball, which remained in place until the advent of Jackie Robinson.

Ernie Banks

E rnie Banks swung a bat like Babe Ruth, had the soft hands of Marty Marion at shortstop, and the saintly disposition of Mother Teresa.

Even Dick Young, the acerbic New York baseball writer whose truculence once drove Tom Seaver to demand a trade from the Mets, had nothing but praise for Mister Cub.

"Ernie Banks," observed Young, "is a beautiful man."

A Dallas native, Banks never played a day in the minor leagues. He joined the Cubs late in 1953 from the Kansas City Monarchs of the Negro American League, and took over as the starting shortstop the following season.

The slender, quick-wristed Banks blossomed into an awesome slugger, compiling 512 career homers. He had a single-season high of 47 in 1958. From 1955 to 1960 Banks out-homered everyone in baseball, including Henry Aaron, Willie Mays, and Mickey Mantle.

He won back-to-back Most Valuable Player Awards in 1958-1959.

A fine fielder, leg injuries curtailed Banks' career as the Cubs shortstop and he shifted to first base. Before moving to first, Banks had a brief, unhappy stint as an outfielder.

When the leg ailments moved him off shortstop late in May 1961, acting manager Vedie Himsl announced Banks would shift to left field. The outfield was strange and lonesome territory for Banks, a career infielder.

"Only a duck out of water could have shared my loneliness in left field," he recalled, claiming he would even agree to become a catcher to escape his exile to the outfield.

A few weeks later, in mid-June, the Cubs installed Banks at first base, where he developed into a terrific gloveman.

B anks and second baseman Gene Baker, another former Kansas City Monarch, were the Cubs' first black players. Baker came to Chicago from Los Angeles of the Pacific Coast League, and he and Banks formed an excellent middle infield combination.

Banks had replaced Baker at shortstop in Kansas City, but the two men met for the first time as members of the Cubs. On their first day of infield practice, Baker offered some advice. "Just watch me," he told Banks, "and everything will be all right."

Banks and Baker became good friends—"He helped me plenty," Ernie recalled—and they roomed together on the road through May 1957, when Baker was traded to Pittsburgh.

On his first day as a Cub, Banks borrowed a bat from slugging outfielder Ralph Kiner, the seven-time N.L. homer king. Stepping up to home plate, Banks sent the first pitch from Cubs coach Roy Johnson into Wrigley Field's left field bleachers.

A crowd had gathered around the batting cage to watch the rookie. After Banks blasted the ball into the bleachers, there was an awed silence that was finally broken by Kiner.

"Hey, Banks," the impressed veteran hollered, "you can use all my bats if you promise to keep on hitting like that!"

Ernie had nothing but praise for his white team-mates on the Cubs, particularly Kiner and another hard-hitting outfielder, Hank Sauer. Banks recalled only one "color"-related incident during his early days in Chicago.

When Ernie joined the Cubs from the Kansas City Monarchs, equipment manager Yosh Kawano noticed the yellow laces on Banks' well-worn baseball shoes. After staring for a moment with a look of disapproval on his face, Kawano bustled off and reappeared with a pair of black shoelaces.

"At the major league level," noted Ernie, "those bright yellow laces were for hot dogs. Yosh wanted to be sure I wouldn't be classed as one."

At the start of his career, Banks used a 33 $\frac{1}{2}$-ounce Babe Ruth-model bat. He eventually switched to a lighter bat, the same model used by Giants outfielder Monte Irvin.

Later in his career, Banks started using a 35", 36-ounce Louisville Slugger, the same type used by Vern "Junior" Stephens, a shortstop with the St. Louis Browns, Red Sox, White Sox, and Orioles from 1941 to 1955.

Ironically, it was Stephens who set the major league record for homers by a shortstop (39, with Boston in 1949) that Banks broke when he hit 44 in 1955.

Leo Durocher was never an Ernie Banks fan when he managed Chicago. Durocher, a member of the notorious St. Louis Cardinals' Gashouse Gang during his playing days, leaned toward more flamboyant players rather than the gentlemanly—although no less competitive—Banks.

"He's too old to play the game anymore," grumbled Durocher after taking the Cubs' reins in 1966, when Ernie was 35.

Durocher's criticism spurred Banks. After a career-low 15-homer, .272 season in '66, Banks bounced back, pounding 23, 32, and 23 round-trippers in his final three seasons as a regular.

Banks spent his entire 19-year career with chronically mediocre Cubs teams. He is one of a handful of Hall of Famers who never had the chance to play in a World Series.

Asked if he had any regrets about not playing for perennial winners like the Yankees or Dodgers, Ernie had this response: "I figure that Ernie Banks is the luckiest person in the world to be associated with the very best organization in baseball—the Chicago Cubs."

B y current standards, the enthusiasm of Ernie Banks seems too good to be true. But Ernie's love of baseball was as genuine as his smile.

"What you saw publicly with Ernie," insists Ron Santo, "was the way he was on the field and in the clubhouse. It wasn't a facade; he truly wanted to play two games every day, three if there had been enough sunshine . . ."

Ross Barnes

Over the years, the Cubs have had their share of power hitters . . . thumpers like Hack Wilson, Rogers Hornsby, Bill Nicholson, Hank Sauer, Ernie Banks, Billy Williams, Ron Santo, Dave Kingman, Andre Dawson, and Sammy Sosa.

It's only fitting, since the man who hit the first homer in National League history wore a Chicago uniform.

When Al Spalding wanted to make Chicago the top team in the newly-formed National League in 1876, he set his sights on Adrian Anson, catcher Deacon White, first sacker Cal McVey, and Ross Barnes.

Spalding and Barnes had known each other for a decade, They'd been teammates on Rockford's Forest Cities clubs, and Henry Chadwick—the true Father of Baseball—described Barnes as "the model second baseman."

Barnes was Chicago's second baseman when the White Stockings played their first game. He was the first batter in team history when he stepped up against Jim Devlin in a game at Louisville on April 25, 1876.

In a May 2 game at Cincinnati, Barnes hit an inside-the-park home run off Reds pitcher Cherokee Bill Fisher in a 15-9 Chicago victory.

Oddly, the dapper-looking infielder's historic homer was the next-to-last of his four-year major league career. Barnes played in an era where home runs were scarce, and his only other round-tripper came in 1879 when he played for the Reds.

Considered by many peers to be the finest player of the Nineteenth Century, Barnes was also the N.L.'s first batting champion.

Glenn Beckert

A lthough the Cubs' Tinker-to-Evers-to-Chance infield is immortalized in verse, the Cubs had another great double play combo from 1965 to 1973 in second baseman Glenn Beckert and shortstop Don Kessinger.

Beckert began his professional career as a shortstop in the Red Sox·organization. When Boston decided Rico Petrocelli was their shortstop of the future, Beckert was left unprotected in the 1962 winter draft.

The Cubs gambled on the Pittsburgh native, and moved him from short to second base in 1964 following the tragic death of Kenny Hubbs.

I n 1965 Beckert replaced journeyman Joey Amalfitano at second base. That same year, Kessinger took the shortstop post from Roberto Pena.

With Kessinger leading off and Beckert in the number-two spot, the Cubs had excellent table-setters for a line-up that included Ernie Banks, Billy Williams, and Ron Santo. Beckert

was an excellent contact hitter who had the fewest strikeouts of any N.L. regular for five straight seasons.

W hen Leo Durocher came to Chicago, he was patient with the Cubs' younger players, including pitcher Ken Holtzman, catcher Randy Hundley, Kessinger, and Beckert. His handling of the younger players helped the Cubs jump from tenth place in 1966 to third in 1967.

Beckert, said Leo, "worked like crazy to improve himself. Made himself into a great player. Another Eddie Stanky."

Durocher helped refine Beckert's game, and the Lip's work paid big dividends. Beckert was a four-time N.L. All-Star, and a Gold Glove winner in 1971.

In 1968 he struck out just 20 times in 643 plate appearances. A lifetime .283 hitter, Beckert batted .342 in 1971. He had hit streaks of 27 consecutive games in 1968 and 26 in '73.

B eckert's roommate during road trips was third sacker Ron Santo, who was a favorite target of clubhouse pranks. Beckert was one of Santo's worst tormentors.

During one stretch when Santo was in a slump, Beckert—together with Ernie Banks and Billy Williams—decided on a remedy to loosen up their buddy.

Beckert, Banks, and Williams found a loud-ticking timer that belonged to the team trainer. They set it for one hour, and placed the timer inside a cardboard box. They disguised the box as fan mail, and then placed it inside Santo's locker.

Later, when Santo strolled into the dressing room and got to his locker, he heard the timer.

"Hey Beck," Santo asked, "do you hear something ticking?"

"Yeah," Beckert said straight-faced. "I've been hearing that ever since I got here." Santo began rummaging through his mail until he found the source of the noise.

"Oh my, it's a bomb!" screamed Santo, heaving the ticking package out the clubhouse window onto Waveland Avenue. Beckert, Banks, and Williams nearly died laughing. Once they came clean, even Santo couldn't keep from cracking up.

The only person who wasn't amused was the Cubs' trainer, once he learned the fate of his timer.

Leg and foot injuries curtailed Beckert's career. Traded to San Diego, he played 73 games for the Padres over the 1974 and '75 seasons and then quit baseball.

Appropriately, Beckert and Don Kessinger played their 1,000th big league game on the same date: August 21, 1971.

Lou Boudreau

L ou Boudreau once came out of the Cubs announce booth to take over as manager. Born in Harvey, Illinois, Boudreau was the son of a former minor league player and a lifelong Cubs fan.

As a youth, Boudreau rooted for the Cubs and attended several games each month at Wrigley Field. His favorite players included Riggs Stephenson, Woody English, Stan Hack, and Billy Jurges.

A s a sophomore, Boudreau sparked his high school team to a state championship. He won an athletic scholarship to the University of Illinois, where he played baseball and basketball. The Cleveland Indians signed Boudreau to his first professional contract in 1938.

An excellent shortstop, Boudreau played for the Indians from 1939 through 1950 and closed out his playing days with the Red Sox in 1951-1952. He was the American League's Most Valuable Player for 1948, hitting a career-high .355.

B oudreau also managed the Indians from 1942 through 1950, guiding the Tribe to the '48 A.L. pennant. He also managed the Red Sox (1952-1954) and Kansas City Athletics (1955-1957) before becoming a Cubs broadcaster.

After Boudreau left Kansas City, announcer Jack Brickhouse urged him to try out for the Cubs broadcast staff on WGN Radio. Boudreau had done a little announcing during his college days, but the transition was daunting—and daring, as well.

"Until then," says Boudreau, "there'd only been a few ex-jocks in broadcasting, which shows you how far ahead of everybody Brickhouse was in 1957. Now every professional announcer has an ex-jock for a partner."

B oudreau auditioned with Brickhouse and WGN sports director Jack Rosenberg as a color man for a simulated game. Boudreau remembers worrying about making grammatical mistakes, or letting fly with some salty dugout language.

But Boudreau's audition was nearly flawless, and Brickhouse and Rosenberg liked what they heard. Boudreau was hired, and his broadcasting career began in 1958.

O n May 4, 1960, the Cubs were wallowing in last place. They'd lost 11 of 17 contests when Cubs vice president Al Holland asked Boudreau to trade places with manager Charlie Grimm.

It was, said one Cubs player, "one of the weirdest transactions in baseball history."

Why Boudreau?

"I think that's obvious," owner Phil Wrigley told the *Chicago Tribune*. "Who else knows the club better than a guy like Lou who's been sitting in the press box for two years? We could have brought in a manager from somewhere else who didn't know the team, but what would have been the sense of that?"

Boudreau agreed to make the switch, and moved the Cubs out of the basement.

At the end of June, Boudreau recalled Ron Santo from the minors and installed the 20-year-old rookie in the starting lineup.

"He'd been a catcher in the minor leagues," says Boudreau, "but I moved him to third base. Don Zimmer, who was nearing the end of his playing career, had been playing that position and helped Santo make the switch—and in effect, helped Santo take Zim's job."

Santo stayed in the Cubs line-up for nearly a decade and a half.

The 1960 Cubs finished seventh, and announced the team would be guided in 1961 by a "College of Coaches"—a rotation system involving Vedie Himsl, Harry Craft, Elvin Tappe, and Lou Klein.

Boudreau declined a berth in the rotation and went back to the broadcast booth. Fans around the league teased the Cubs about the new system. On road trips, they'd taunt whomever was in charge at the time with lines like:

"When are you going to call a classroom meeting and paddle your boys?" or, "What's going to happen next week when you're not here?"

Years later, reliever Don Elston looked back on the experiment with disdain.

"There was jealousy among the coaches," Elston told the *Chicago Tribune.* "When one guy was head coach, some but not all of the other coaches did nothing to help him. They sat there waiting for their turn. It was an unhappy time."

The Cubs lost 193 games over the next two seasons and went back to a single field boss in 1963, when Chicago native Bob Kennedy took over.

B oudreau was elected to the Hall of Fame in 1970. His son Jim was a left-hander who pitched in the College World Series for Arizona State and spent a couple of years in the Cubs' chain.

Boudreau's son-in-law, former big league pitching star Denny McLain, was the 1968 A.L. MVP.

Lou Brock

The 1964 trade that sent outfielder Lou Brock from Chicago to St. Louis is considered one of the worst in Cubs history. The truth is, Brock's performance in Chicago gave no indication of his future greatness—even when he played in the Windy City in 1959, two years before joining the Cubs.

For most Chicago fans, the less said the better when it comes to the trade that sent Brock to the Cardinals along with pitchers Jack Spring and Paul Toth for outfielder Doug Clemens and pitchers Bobby Shantz and Ernie Broglio. Clemens batted .238 for Chicago from '64 through 1965. Shantz was 0-1 in 20 games as a Cub and Broglio, a 21-game winner for the Cardinals in 1960, was 7-19 between '64 and 1966.

While Toth and Spring made marginal contributions in St. Louis, Brock went on to become one of the greatest base stealers of all time. In 1985 he was inducted into the Hall of Fame.

B ut Brock's brief sojourn with the Cubs gave no hint of what was to come.

True, he'd batted .361 for St. Cloud to lead the Northern League in 1961, his first year as a professional. But in his first two complete seasons in Wrigley Field, he hit .243 and .269. Brock was averaging .251 when the Cubs sent him packing. Of his career total of 938 stolen bases, just 50 came in a Chicago uniform.

O nce before, Brock had been a bust in Chicago. It happened two years before his pro debut.

As a Southern University sophomore in 1959, Brock's .545 batting average led the Southwest Athletic Conference. The Jaguars won the NAIA title, and Brock was named to the United States team for the Pan American Games.

The Pan Ams took place that year in Chicago, and the American squad finished third behind Venezuela and Puerto Rico. Brock had just one hit in 10 trips to the plate.

I n the first two decades after World War Two, it was said that everyone in Chicago stole . . . except the Cubs. Brock pilfered 16 bases in his first year in Chicago, and 23 the next.

He could run all right, but nothing else seemed to go right for the youngster.

"He'd break out in a big sweat just putting on his uniform," recalled Cubs pitcher Larry Jackson. "His desire was so intense that he made things tough for himself."

" If you have watched all the Cub home games thus far," noted a Chicago sportswriter in April 1963, "you probably have come to the conclusion that Lou Brock is the worst outfielder in baseball history. He really isn't, but he hasn't done much to prove it."

Years later, Brock would look back and say the criticism was "a mite harsh," but he owned up to having trouble with left-handers and grounders ("he hand-fought ground balls," observed one scribe).

"The coaches would get me out to Wrigley Field at 8 a.m. every day," says Brock, "practice all morning long and then—after that—I'd have nothing left for the game."

Brock did have one moment of greatness as a Cub, and it had nothing to do with running the bases.

During his 19-year big league career, Brock hit just 149 home runs. Against the Mets on June 17, 1962, however, Brock homered an estimated 475 feet into the right-center field bleachers at the Polo Grounds.

Al Jackson was on the hill for New York, and the little lefty had whiffed Brock twice that afternoon. Ernie Banks, who was Brock's roommate, had been after him to relax.

" When you walk up to the plate," Mr. Cub would tell the youngster, "there's really only three factors involved: you, the pitcher, and the ball. Once the ball is released, there's only two factors: you and the ball. And heck, Lou, the ball is just a round, hard piece of horsehide, but you are a man with a bat in your hands and good eyes in your head."

A fter striking out twice against Jackson in the 1962 game at the Polo Grounds, Brock was just hoping to make contact.

Jackson delivered a curve, high and outside. Brock swung and connected. He felt the bat meet the ball, and took off. Brock saw the ball streaming toward cavernous center field in the Polo Grounds, and Mets' outfielder Richie Ashburn running with his back to the infield.

With visions of a three-base hit dancing in his head, Brock turned on the jets. When he saw home plate umpire Tom Gorman giving the home run signal, Brock thought it meant he had a chance for an inside-the-park homer. Brock circled the bases in a flash, but as he rounded home he saw the Mets catcher just standing there.

Not until after he'd crossed the plate did Brock discover he'd driven the ball into the farthest recesses of the Polo Grounds. Only two other big league batters—Babe Ruth and Joe Adcock—had ever reached that spot.

Jim Brosnan

A pitcher for the Cubs from 1954 to 1958, right-hander Jim Brosnan authored two classic baseball books: *The Long Season* (a chronicle of Brosnan's 1960 season with Cincinnati) and *Pennant Race* (a first-person account of the Reds' first-place finish in 1961).

After retiring in 1963, he became a full-time writer.

Known as "The Professor," Brosnan was a student of the game . . . and also of human nature. He once offered a classic observation on big league coaching staffs.

"All coaches," Brosnan wryly pointed out, "religiously carry fungo bats in the spring to ward off suggestions that they are not working."

Three-Finger Brown

There are two monuments that commemorate the pitching career of Cubs great Mordecai Peter Centennial Brown. One is in Cooperstown, New York, site of baseball's Hall of Fame. The other is about four hours south of Chicago in the coal mining town of Nyesville, Indiana, some 35 miles north of Terre Haute.

Brown, elected to the Hall of Fame in 1974 with a career record of 239-139, was the nemesis of Ty Cobb and Christy Mathewson, two other Cooperstown honorees.

Cobb called Brown's curve "the most devastating pitch I've ever faced."

A farm accident when Brown was seven years old mangled his right hand. When he tried pitching, he found his disfigured

digits put an unhittable spin on the ball. Brown reached the majors with the Cardinals in 1903 and was traded to the Cubs a year later. He won 20 or more games from 1906-1911, including a 29-game season in 1908.

Brown helped the Cubs to pennants from 1906 through '08, and a pair of World Series triumphs in '07-'08. Backed by the legendary Tinker-to-Evers-to-Chance infield, Brown's 26 victories in 1906 led a Cubs staff that won 116 games—a major league record that still stands.

D uring Brown's era, the Giants and Cubs were fierce rivals. The great Christy Mathewson, winner of 373 major league contests, was New York's top hurler. Brown and Matty squared off 24 times. Brown won 13 of those games, including nine in a row from July 12, 1905, to October 8, 1908.

The great Mathewson heaped praise on his Chicago rival. Brown, said Matty, "is a finished pitcher in all departments of the game. Besides being a great worker, he is a wonderful fielder and sure death on bunts. He spends weeks in the spring preparing himself to field short hits in the infield, and it is fatal to try to bunt against him."

B rown won five World Series contests, including a 2-0 triumph over Detroit in the fifth and decisive game of the 1907 World Series. Prior to the Series, Cobb had boasted that he would "hit .800 against National League pitching."

The first time Cobb faced Brown, he struck out on four

pitches. Cobb batted .200 in the Series. In four at-bats against Brown, he struck out twice.

B rown played for the Reds and with Federal League teams in St. Louis, Brooklyn, and Chicago from 1913 to 1915 before returning to the Cubs.

He left the big leagues after the 1916 season. For a time, he was field boss of the St. Louis team, making him the last full-time pitcher to manage a major league ball club.

T eammate Jimmy Archer recalled how Brown's precision control earned the respect of a legendary N.L. arbiter.

"One time I was warming up Brown, and Bill Klem, the umpire, pushed me aside," Archer reminisced. "He put a piece of paper the size of a half dollar on the ground. 'That's the only target that fellow needs to pitch to,' Klem said. And he was right."

D uring the winter of 1912-1913, after he'd jumped leagues, Brown took a suite at the Missouri Athletic Club in St. Louis. A fire swept through the hotel, killing several guests. At first, Brown was believed to be among the victims.

Like Mark Twain, however, reports of his death had been greatly exaggerated. Brown's wife Sallie had come to town and, since the MAC was a men-only club, they'd booked a room at the American Hotel. Brown lost his personal effects but, fortunately, wasn't around for the fire.

Known as "Three Finger," "Miner," and "Brownie" around the big leagues, Brown was just plain Mort back in western Indiana. After his playing days were over he settled in Terre Haute, operating a filling station there.

Fifty years after his death on Valentine's Day 1948, the citizens of Nyesville erected a marker in Brown's honor in a cornfield on what was once his boyhood homestead.

Harry Caray

H oly Cow!
Love him or hate him, Harry Caray was as much a part of the Cubs as ivy vines and daytime baseball. His out-of-tune rendition of *Take Me Out to the Ballgame* during each seventh-inning stretch at Wrigley Field and his gleeful call of "Cubs win! Cubs win!" after each Chicago triumph irritated some and delighted others.

When it came to his team, Harry could never be accused of being impartial. Whether he was announcing for the Cardinals, A's, White Sox, or Cubs, Caray was his ball club's No. 1 cheerleader.

And, during his years in the Wrigley Field broadcast booth, Harry Caray was the Cubs.

H arry was the first of three generations of broadcasters. Skip Caray, Harry's son, handles Braves telecasts.

Skip's son, Chip Caray, started out with Atlanta and moved to the Cubs in 1997.

S ome of Caray's most colorful lines had nothing to do with baseball commentary. The Cubs once had an attractive ball girl named Marla Collins, who posed for Playboy.

After seeing Collins in the magazine, Harry pronounced: "That's the best thing I've seen out of uniform this year!"

C aray's first marriage ended in divorce in 1949.

"I never realized how short a month is," he once quipped, "until I started paying alimony."

When Harry sent a payment to his ex-wife on the 30th anniversary of their split, he enclosed a note.

"Holy Cow!" it said. "Thirty years. How much longer does this go on?"

A week later, Caray got a note from his ex. It read: "Dear Harry, Till death do us part!"

Jose Cardenal

In an 18-year big league career, Cuban-born outfielder Jose Cardenal played for nine teams. He spent 1972 through 1977 with Chicago.

As the Cubs' right fielder in 1973, he led the team with a .303 average and was voted Chicago Player of the Year by Windy City baseball writers. Cardenal batted .296 during his six-season run as a Cubbie.

Cardenal was involved in a memorable "brawl" during a 1982 Spring Training game with the Giants. When the skirmish broke out, Cardenal headed straight for San Francisco's Willie McCovey.

"I want you, big man," barked the 5' 10", 150-pound Cardenal at the massive first baseman, but from a considerable distance. Cardenal then leaped up and threw a punch at his 6' 4", 225-pound opponent . . . and missed by about a foot.

Even McCovey had to laugh.

One year, a bizarre malady forced Cardenal out of the Cubs' Opening Day line-up: one of his eyelids was stuck shut!

Don Cardwell

Some Cubs fans can never forgive Don Cardwell for helping the Mets blow past Chicago en route to the 1969 N.L. pennant. But long before the right-hander pitched for New York, he was a durable star for the Cubs.

The rangy North Carolinian broke in with the Phillies in 1957 and joined the Cubs on May 13, 1960, in a four-player trade that brought Cardwell and first baseman Ed Bouchee to Chicago in return for second baseman Tony Taylor and catcher Cal Neeman.

Two days later at Wrigley Field, manager Lou Boudreau sent Cardwell to the mound to start the second game of a double-header with the Cardinals. Cardwell walked the second St. Louis batter, shortstop Alex Grammas, then retired the next 23 straight Cardinals.

In the top of the ninth inning Carl Sawatski, a former Cub who'd been Cardwell's batterymate in Philadelphia, entered the

game as a pinch hitter. On an 0-2 count, Sawatski blasted Cardwell's next offering deep to right.

Anticipating an extra base hit, the Sunday crowd of 33,543 let out a collective groan. The fans cheered a moment later as right fielder George Altman, running at full tilt, leaped in the air at the exit gate at the bend of the bleachers for a dramatic, one-handed catch.

One out later right fielder Joe Cunningham strode to the plate. A .324 hitter, Cunningham was all that stood between Cardwell and a no-hitter. Cunning-ham worked the count to 3-1, then sliced a low liner to left. Walt "Moose" Moryn lumbered in and made a breathtaking, shoestring catch to end the game.

The Cubs won 4-0, and Cardwell had thrown a no-hitter in his first appearance for his new team, a feat no other major league pitcher had accomplished.

"All I wanted was to get out there and win so the Cubs would be impressed with their trade for me," said Cardwell, who was mobbed by fans after the final out.

Cardwell was even more impressive in 1961, registering 15 of the Cubs' 64 wins. Traded to St. Louis after the 1962 season, Cardwell moved on to Pittsburgh and later the Mets before ending his career with the Braves in 1970.

At 33, Cardwell was the old man of a youthful Mets' pitching staff in 1969 which included Tom Seaver, Jerry Koosman, and Nolan Ryan.

Cardwell's 1960 no-hitter wasn't his only shining moment that season. His other noteworthy performance took place September 2, also at the expense of the Cardinals. Cardwell not only struck out nine batters in a 10-4 complete-game win at St. Louis, he also cracked a pair of homers.

It marked only the 24th time in 85 N.L. seasons that a pitcher had hit two homers in a single contest.

Phil Cavarretta

H onesty may be the best policy, but it cost Phil Cavarretta
his job as manager of the Cubs.

B orn in Chicago to Sicilian immigrant parents, Cavarretta
starred in baseball at Lane Tech. He signed his first pro
contract in 1934 at 17 years of age. He played seven games for
the Cubs at the tail end of the season.

In 1935 Chicago manager Charlie Grimm, who'd pla-
tooned himself at first base the previous year, turned over the post
to Cavarretta. The wispy 18-year-old hit .275 as the Cubs won
the N.L. flag.

Cavarretta played on two more pennant winners in 1938
and 1945. He hit .355 in '45, becoming the Cubs' first batting
champ since Heinie Zimmerman in 1912. Versus Detroit in the
World Series he batted .423.

Some of the credit for Cavarretta's 1945 batting title should have gone to New York Giants pitcher Sal Maglie.

All season long, Cavarretta waged a nip-and-tuck battle for the batting crown with Tommy Holmes of the Braves. Holmes set a modern N.L. record that season by hitting in 37 straight games, a record that stood until Cincinnati's Pete Rose hit in 44 straight in 1978.

Maglie, a rookie in 1945, earned the nickname "The Barber" for the close shaves he gave any batter who crowded the plate while he was pitching. Whenever he pitched against the Braves, Maglie would send Holmes sprawling in the dirt.

Years, later, the scowling right-hander revealed that he had done all he could to help Cavarretta, a fellow *paisan.*

"If *you* were Italian," Maglie told Holmes, "I wouldn't have decked you so many times."

It was the irrepressible Charlie Grimm who gave the Cubs first sacker his nickname.

"When I first saw Cavarretta back there in the mid-'30s," Grimm recollected, "I started calling him 'Philibuck.' It just came to me and was inspired, if you can call it that, by my reaction that here was a hard-nosed athlete. Phil liked it."

Bill Nicholson, a teammate from 1939 through 1948, described Cavarretta as a "fiery ballplayer, and a good one."

"He was high strung, both on and off the field," Nicholson remembered. "It didn't take much to get him stirred up, but he was a nice fellow all the same."

After the war, the Cubs began a slow, downhill slide. They finished in last place three of four seasons between 1948 and 1951. Cavarretta replaced Frank Frisch as manager during the '51 season, and the Cubs moved up to fifth place in '52 with a 77-77 record.

Injuries, a dried-up farm system and disastrous trades (including a deal with Brooklyn in '51 that cost them their best all-around hitter, center fielder Andy Pafko) had taken a toll. With slugger Hank Sauer missing one-third of the '53 season with an injured hand, the Cubs wound up seventh.

In 1954 the Cubs went to Spring Training in Mesa, Arizona. Cavarretta saw a future star in Ernie Banks and had a few other capable players in camp. The pitching was weak, however, and after two decades in baseball Cavarretta knew what lay in store for the Cubs.

In late March, the 36-year-old player-manager gave owner Phil Wrigley a frank assessment of the ballclub. "They can't win," Cavarretta told his boss.

On March 29 the owner made a shocking move. With the Cubs in Dallas to play the Giants, Wrigley replaced Cavarretta with Stan Hack. Cavarretta, stated Cubs officials, had been guilty of "negative thinking."

Offered the managerial post at Los Angeles in the P.C.L., the disgruntled Cavarretta—who had become the first manager to be fired during Spring Training—left the squad and signed to play for the crosstown White Sox.

"I thought it was my duty to tell the truth," he told reporters.

Cavarretta was indeed telling the truth. The '54 Cubs finished seventh, 33 games out of first place. The only regular pitcher with a winning mark was Jim Davis (11-7), who joined the Cubs after Cavarretta's departure.

Cavarretta, the Cubs' last link to the glory days of Gabby Hartnett, Billy Jurges, Billy Herman, and Chuck Klein, batted .316 as a part-timer for the Sox. After retiring in 1955, he managed in the minors and scouted, and was a successful batting instructor in the Mets' system.

"Phil was the best manager I ever played for," said Frankie Baumholtz, a Cubs outfielder from 1949 to 1955. "He always spoke his piece. But he knew baseball."

Chuck Connors

C huck Connors is best remembered as television's Lucas
McCain, the Winchester-toting hero of *The Rifleman,*
which aired on ABC from 1958 to 1963. Before that, however,
the rangy Connors was a pro athlete in two sports.

B orn and raised in Brooklyn, New York, Connors was a high
school baseball and basketball standout.

In November 1946 he made professional basketball history
with the Boston Celtics. Warming up for a preseason game with
the Chicago Stags at Boston Arena, the 6' 5", 190-pound
Connors tried to dunk the ball. Instead he managed to shatter
the glass backboard. It was the first time in pro basketball history
that a player had smashed a backboard, and arena officials
didn't have a replacement.

Celtics publicist Howie McHugh saved the day by arrang-
ing to borrow Boston Garden's backboard.

After quitting basketball in 1948, Connors joined the Brooklyn Dodgers in 1949 and had one at-bat as a pinch hitter. He grounded into a double play.

According to legend, Connors passed first base and kept on running.

"Hey, Connors," hollered Brooklyn first base coach Jake Pitler, "where ya goin'?"

Still on the run in the direction of the team clubhouse, Connors shot back: "To Montreal!"

After the game, that's exactly where the Dodgers shipped Connors—to their farm club north of the border in Quebec Province.

In 1950 the Dodgers peddled Connors to the Cubs along with fellow first baseman Dee Fondy in return for catcher Hank Edwards.

Although sorry to leave his native Brooklyn, Connors wasn't sad about getting away from Branch Rickey, the parsimonious Dodger general manager.

"Rickey had both money and players," quipped Connors. "He just didn't like to see the two of them mixed."

For most of his time in the Chicago chain, Connors played for Los Angeles of the Pacific Coast League.

In 1951 he batted .321 with 22 homers for the Angels before moving up to Chicago, where he batted .239 in 66 games.

B ack with Los Angeles in 1952, Connors landed a bit part in the film *Pat and Mike,* starring Spencer Tracy and Katherine Hepburn.

The lanky Connors was bitten by the acting bug. He began entertaining teammates and opposing players alike by quoting Shakespeare on the ballfield. In the clubhouse, he would break into dramatic recitations of *Casey at the Bat* at the slightest provocation.

After the '52 season Connors hung up his spikes, concentrating on what would prove to be a long career in film and television.

"He didn't have to play baseball anymore," quipped third baseman Randy Jackson, Connors' teammate in Chicago during the 1951 campaign, "because he became a successful actor."

Jimmy Cooney

Some 60,000 total fans flocked to Forbes Field for a Pirates-Cubs double-header on May 30, 1927. They wound up getting their money's worth:

• Five future Hall of Famers were in the starting line-ups: Pie Traynor and the Waner brothers, Paul and Lloyd, for Pittsburgh, plus Hack Wilson and Gabby Hartnett for the Cubs.

• Both contests were decided by one run in extra innings. After dropping the morning game 7-6 in 10 innings, the Bucs came back to win the afternoon contest, 6-5, in 10.

• In the first game, the Cubs broke an 11-game win streak by Pittsburgh, the eventual N.L. pennant winner.

But the most unforgettable moment came in the first game, when Jimmy Cooney of the Cubs pulled off an unassisted triple play.

Cooney's dad, Jimmy Sr., had played for Chicago in the early 1890s. Both father and son were good-fielding, light-hitting shortstops.

Jimmy Jr. joined the Cubs in 1926 after stints with the Braves, Giants, and Cardinals. In '26, Cooney's only full year with the Cubs, he topped N.L. shortstops in fielding and double plays.

In the fourth inning of the first game of the '27 double-header at Pittsburgh, the Pirates had Lloyd Waner at second base and Clyde Barnhart on first.

Paul Waner, the next batter, hit a line drive that Cooney snared for the first out. Going to his left, Cooney stepped on second to retire Lloyd Waner. Barnhart, off at the crack of the bat, was a dead duck as Cooney took a few more steps and tagged him out.

The fielding gem was Cooney's last great moment with the Cubs. Just eight days later, on June 7, 1927, he was traded to the Phillies. Woody English, a Chicago rookie in '27, took Cooney's place.

"Jimmy had some age on him," said English, explaining the deal. "He was a slick fielder, but not much of an all-around athlete. Couldn't run much."

Kiki Cuyler

Kiki Cuyler was a devout Catholic who often made the sign of the cross prior to stepping into the batter's box—a rare sight in the '20s and '30s, prior to the proliferation of Latin ballplayers.

"Judging from his record," notes one Cubs historian, "it must have worked."

Cuyler, a Hall of Fame outfielder, hit .321 in 18 big league seasons, and .325 in eight years as a Cub. Cuyler's career began with the Pirates in 1921.

He came to the Cubs under unusual circumstances following the 1927 season.

B y the mid-'20s, Cuyler was well-established as Pittsburgh's left fielder. Two years earlier, he'd been runner-up to Rogers Hornsby in the MVP ballot.

In 1927, former Tiger shortstop Donie Bush took over as manager of the Pirates. In June, Bush moved Cuyler from the number-three spot in the batting order to second. Cuyler, a top RBI man, wasn't happy with the switch.

When he failed to deliver, Cuyler asked Bush to move him back to third. The situation led to hard feelings between the two men. When Cuyler failed to slide on a force play at second, the irascible Bush benched him.

The media and fans entered the fray, siding with Cuyler. Bush, however, wouldn't budge. Cuyler appeared in just 85 games, and during the World Series he rode the bench as the Yankees took apart Pittsburgh in four games.

After the season the Pirates shipped him to the Cubs for infielder Sparky Adams and outfielder Pete Scott.

It was one of the best trades in Chicago history. Had Bush kept Cuyler, he would have had three Hall of Fame outfielders in Cuyler and the Waner brothers, Paul, and Lloyd.

W ith the Cubs, Cuyler teamed with Hack Wilson and Riggs Stephenson to form one of the best-hitting outfield combinations of all time. Yet Cuyler remained aloof.

"He was a loner," observed shortstop Woody English. "He kept to himself. He liked to dance, and he'd go out, never palled around with a single player on the club. They didn't really dislike him, but he wasn't one of the boys."

Cuyler had a career-best .360 average for the 1929 Cubs and led the N.L. in stolen bases three years in a row.

He moved on to Cincinnati in 1935 and finished his playing days with Brooklyn in 1938.

Jim Davis

J im Davis was a southpaw pitcher with the Cubs from 1954 to 1956. His playing days ended after he spent the 1957 season with the Cardinals and Giants. Davis was 24-26 with a career earned run average of 4.01, but he made the record book . . . the hard way.

A s a rookie in '54, Davis was 11-7 for the seventh-place Cubs with a staff-leading 3.52 ERA.

He wasn't the first member of his family to pitch in the majors. Jim's uncle, right-hander Marv Grissom, hurled for five teams from 1946 to 1959.

On May 27, 1956, the Cubs were in St. Louis for a double header at old Busch Stadium. Davis was Chicago's first-game starting pitcher.

In the bottom of the sixth, Davis struck out Hal Smith for the first out. Jackie Brandt went down on strikes for out number two, and Davis fanned Cards pitcher Lindy McDaniel for what appeared to be the third out.

McDaniel, however, made it safely to first base when Cubs catcher Hobie Landrith couldn't hold on to the ball. Davis then fanned Don Blasingame for the final out—and fourth strikeout—of the inning.

Davis was the first N.L. pitcher in half a century to strike out four batters in a single inning. Prior to Davis, the last hurler to perform the feat was Hooks Wiltse of the Giants against Cincinnati in 1906.

And for the record: the Cubs went on to lose to the Cardinals, 11-9.

They also dropped the nightcap, 12-2.

Andre Dawson

Anyone who saw a game at Wrigley Field between 1987 and 1992 remembers the drill: The Hawk trots to his outfield post. Fans in the right field bleachers stand and bow. They add a "salaam" motion, with right arms outstretched.

Andre "Hawk" Dawson, the Cubs right fielder from 1987 to 1992, was one of the most beloved players in Chicago history. How he came to play in Chicago goes back to his high school days.

As a prep in Miami, Dawson played defensive back on the school football team. While trying to make an interception, Dawson suffered a knee injury that would bother him throughout his athletic career.

He came to the major leagues with the Expos, and Dawson won the 1977 N.L. Rookie of the Year Award. He enjoyed an outstanding 10-year run in Montreal.

Years of play on Olympic Stadium's synthetic turf caused his leg to ache, however, and by 1984 Dawson was taking pain pills. When he got out of bed on mornings after a game, Dawson had to hobble into the shower and run hot water on his legs in order to move around.

Until the 1986 season, Dawson prided himself on his ability to play despite the agony. But that year, Dawson recalls, "I could think about nothing else but the throbbing pain in my knees. I was beginning to feel like an old man. I walked like old Festus from the TV show *Gunsmoke*."

After the 1986 season Dawson became a free agent. His good friend and former Expos teammate Warren Cromartie, who by then played for the Yomiuri Giants in Tokyo, tried to convince Dawson to come to Japan.

"They'll pay you the real money that you deserve over here," insisted Cromartie.

But Dawson's wife Vanessa had other ideas, especially after all the years she and Andre had spent in French-speaking Quebec.

"You're crazy!" she informed Dawson. "Both of you are crazy! Playing ball in Japan? It's bad enough that we would speak differently from all the hundreds of millions of people over there, but we'd look different, too!"

And so Dawson set his sights instead on Wrigley Field, a hitter's paradise with natural grass. The Cubs seemed reluctant, so Dawson made an unprecedented offer. Send a blank contract, said Hawk, and I'll sign it; you fill in the dollar amount.

Pitcher Rick Sutcliffe offered to donate $100,000 of his own salary to sign Dawson. "We got no chance to win without him," maintained Sut. "And it would be worth it to me to get him on our club."

The Cubs signed Dawson for $500,000, less than half his salary at Montreal. Yet he couldn't have been happier.

"I was a Chicago Cub!" Dawson remembers thinking. "I wanted to jump, I wanted to scream."

When he batted for the first time in Chicago, the Wrigley Field fans gave him a standing ovation.

If the '87 Cubs couldn't win without Dawson, they didn't win with him, either. They finished last in the N.L. East.

But Dawson was a one-man show. He became the first player from a last-place club to capture the MVP Award, driving in 137 runs with 47 homers and a .287 batting average. Chicago rooters had found a new hero.

"Everything was too good to be true," says Dawson of his first year in Chicago, "especially the Cubbie fans. I could talk, mix, and have a relationship with them, something I had been unable to do in Montreal."

Dawson was part of Chicago's resurgence in 1989 under manager Don Zimmer. The Cubs improved by 16 games to finish ahead of the Mets, N.L. champions a year before. Against all odds, the "Boys of Zimmer" won the Eastern Division title.

Dawson's knee had started acting up again, and he underwent surgery in May. Despite playing in just 118 games, he still managed 21 homers and 77 RBI.

But once again, the Cubs were thwarted in post-season play when the Giants beat them in the League Championship Series.

D awson left the Cubs after 1992 and played for Boston and Miami before retiring. Like so many other Cub greats, his days in Wrigley Field were unforgettable.

"In Montreal," he reminisced, "you never got quite the exposure you get here in the States. In Chicago, you became a household name. The fans love the ball club and are right on top of you. It makes it easy to go out and enjoy yourself."

A deeply religious man, Dawson made an impact not only on the game, but on many of his fellow players.

"He inspired others by who he is and the example he sets," declares Ernie Banks. "All who touch his life, just by his example, better who they are."

Leon Durham

Leon Durham played for the Cubs from 1981 to 1988. He came to Chicago after the 1980 season along with third baseman Ken Reitz and infielder-outfielder Tye Waller from St. Louis for relief pitcher Bruce Sutter.

Prior to the 1984 campaign, Durham tried two changes . . . with opposite results.

During Spring Training that year, Durham switched from glasses to contact lenses. He had trouble with contacts, however, claiming that he "wasn't really seeing what I should see."

Durham switched back to glasses, and felt more comfortable with them.

"I was very relaxed," he says, "and confident of what the pitchers were throwing at me."

Durham went on to clout 33 homers and knock in 99 runs that season. He wore glasses the rest of his career.

D urham also switched from the outfield to first base at the Cubs 1984 spring camp. He had suffered a series of leg injuries in 1983—due in part, Durham maintained, to lugging his 6' 3", 215-pound frame around the outfield.

Cubs' management also felt Durham's arm was below average for the outfield, and that he'd be better suited to an infield role.

"I thought Leon would be better at first base," said manager Jim Frey after incumbent Bill Buckner was swapped to Boston to make room for Durham. "And so far I've been right."

Durham concurred.

"I don't think I was that good of an outfielder," he admitted.

Durham manned first base in Wrigley Field until the arrival of Mark Grace in 1988.

G rowing up in Cincinnati, Durham enjoyed watching the Reds at old Crosley Field. His heroes were Pete Rose, Frank Robinson, Vada Pinson, and Tony Perez.

He didn't get to go to the 1970 All-Star Game at Riverfront Stadium, but watched on television as Rose scored the winning run in the bottom of the 12th.

When Durham himself was elected to the N.L. All-Star team in 1982, the honor was especially gratifying.

"Chills actually went through my body" he says, "when I learned I'd been named to the National League team."

Durham got his hands on his first big league baseball at Crosley Field. He beat out 10 other youngsters in a race for the ball, making a bare-handed stop in the process.

Years later, fond memories of his boyhood days at the ballpark prompted Durham to donate $500 to athletic programs in Chicago-area schools each time he hit a home run.

Frank Ernaga's Big Debut

Everyone deserves 15 minutes of fame, theorized Andy Warhol, but Frank Ernaga's renown lasted about three innings.

At Wrigley Field on May 24, 1957, the Cubs trailed the Milwaukee Braves 1-0 going into the home half of the second inning. Rookie right fielder Frank Ernaga, recalled from Portland of the Pacific Coast League just four days earlier, led off the inning against future Hall of Famer Warren Spahn.

The ex-UCLA star worked the count to 2-1 before whacking Spahn's next pitch into the left-center field stands. Ernaga's homer not only tied the score, it put him in the record book: he was the first Cub to hit a home run in his initial major league at-bat.

After Jim Bolger led off the fourth with a single, Ernaga batted again. This time he lined a low drive toward center that skipped past Billy Bruton. By the time Bruton got the ball back to the infield, Ernaga was on third with a triple. Moments later, Ernaga scored on Cal Neeman's sacrifice fly.

The Cubs went on to win 5-1 behind 21-year-old right-hander Moe Drabowsky. Ernaga had homered and tripled in his first two major league plate appearances.

In his brief major league career, nothing before or after matched that awesome debut.

With Tulsa of the Texas League in 1956, Ernaga had 18 homers and 97 RBI. He was batting .252 for Portland when the Cubs promoted him, looking for additional bench power.

Not long after obtaining outfielder Chuck Tanner from the Braves on June 8, the Cubs dispatched Ernaga to Fort Worth of the Texas League. Ernaga's slate with the '57 Cubs showed a .314 batting average with two homers and a pair of triples.

The gaudy numbers, however, don't tell the full story. A contemporary scouting report indicated Ernaga had "plenty of power, though weak on curve balls."

Defensively, he was something of a liability.

"Shows good hands and arm," the report continued, "but covers very little ground. May be tried as catcher."

At Fort Worth, Ernaga batted .238 in 89 contests. He returned there in 1958, hitting .249 with 10 homers.

Ernaga briefly resurfaced with the Cubs in '58 and batted .125 in nine games before disappearing from the major leagues forever. His career slate shows a .278 average, two triples, and a pair of homers.

Ernaga eventually returned to Susanville, California, his birthplace, and became a building contractor.

Bill Faul

The Cubs have had their share of characters and oddballs . . . maybe more than their share.

Few rank ahead of Bill Faul.

Faul was a right-handed pitcher who broke in with Detroit in 1962. Tiger teammates claimed Faul had "problems" and would occasionally go wild on the mound.

In an effort to calm himself down and concentrate on his pitching, Faul visited a psychiatrist. The doctor recommended self-hypnosis.

"But it didn't seem to work," said Detroit infielder Coot Veal. "He had good stuff, but was in a different world. He wasn't dangerous, just different. Players stayed away from him."

The Cubs purchased Faul's contract just prior to the 1965 season. In the locker room prior to his first start, Faul unnerved his new teammates when he produced a small record player and played a disc that said, over and over:

"You're going to keep the baaaaaaalllllll dowwwwwwwn, you're going to keep the baaaaaaalllllll dowwwwwwwn. You're going to pitch loooooooowwwww and awaaaaaaay, loooooooowwwww and awaaaaaaay."

As the record played, Faul went into a trance. When the record finished, Faul would snap out of it, pumped up and ready for action.

"He was ready to play all nine positions of a double-header himself," mused Ron Santo.

Faul posted a 6-6 record in his first year with the Cubs, including three shutout victories. He was gone the following year when he slipped to 1-4.

The remaining Cubs probably breathed a collective sigh of relief.

Dee Fondy

Dee Fondy was an anomaly. A big man at 6' 3", 195 pounds, he was an excellent base runner, adept at the drag bunt. Yet he didn't hit with the power of other good-sized first basemen of the '50s, like Dale Long or Joe Adcock.

A notorious streak hitter, Fondy's first major league at-bat was an unforgettable one.

The Texas-born, California-bred Fondy had served as an artilleryman in Europe during World War Two, earning a Purple Heart. Fondy's professional baseball career didn't begin until 1946, when he was nearly 22 years old.

Fondy signed with the Dodgers. With Gil Hodges playing first base for Brooklyn, however, Fondy languished in the minors.

B y 1950, longtime Cubs first sacker Phil Cavarretta was showing signs of wear. After a broken arm shelved Cavarretta, Preston Ward inherited the job. Ward batted .253 in 80 games for the '50 Cubs, but then entered military service.

A few weeks after the season ended, the Cubs acquired Fondy and Chuck Connors, another first baseman, in a trade with Brooklyn.

T he left-handed Fondy made the 1951 Cubs squad as a 26-year-old rookie. His first major league at-bat left a big impression on Cubs fans.

On a sunny but chilly Opening Day, April 17, the Cubs hosted the Reds at Wrigley Field. Chicago manager Frank Frisch started Fondy at first base, batting sixth behind Andy Pafko.

Kenny Raffensberger was the Reds starter. The left-hander was a notorious Chicago-killer who had won his last six starts against the Cubs.

When Fondy batted in the first inning, the bases were loaded with two out. Frank Baumholtz was on third, Hank Sauer on second, and Pafko aboard at first. To the delight of 18,211 fans, Fondy whacked a triple.

He followed with two singles in his next three at-bats. Fondy's 3-for-4 performance and four RBI helped the Cubs to an 8-3 victory.

T hrough his first 49 games Fondy batted .271. Frisch turned over first base duties to Chuck Connors and optioned Fondy to Los Angeles of the Pacific Coast League. While the future TV and film star batted just .239 for the Cubs, Fondy pasted P.C.L. pitching at a .376 clip and reclaimed his starting role in 1952.

"Fondy burned up the P.C.L.," says Randy Jackson, a Cubs third baseman in 1951, "and Connors couldn't hit major league pitching. So they swapped them in the middle of the year, and Connors did great in the P.C.L. and Fondy had a bad first year with the Cubs."

During his years in Chicago, Fondy showed signs of greatness. His best season as a Cub was 1953, when he hit .309 with 18 homers. Fondy legged out 11 triples in 53 and stole 20 bases in 1954—the highest Cubs total since Stan Hack's 21 in 1940.

Fondy held down the first base post at Wrigley Field until May of 1957, when he was traded to Pittsburgh. Dealt by the Pirates to Cincinnati for Ted Kluszewski following the '57 season, Dee retired after 1958.

As a hitter, Fondy seemed to be red-hot or ice-cold. He once struck out six times during a July 1953 double-header, five times in a single contest.

In 1954, with 25 games to go, Fondy was batting just .266. He then caught fire, hitting at a .383 clip the rest of the way to finish at .285. He averaged .286 for his eight-year big league career, and .285 as a Cub.

Fondy held several jobs in baseball after his playing days, including a stretch as special assistant to the general manager of the Milwaukee Brewers.

Ray Fontenot

Silton Ray Fontenot, a left-handed pitcher from Lake Charles, Louisiana, came to the Cubs in December 1984 as part of a six-player deal with the Yankees. He won nine and lost 15 in Chicago before the Cubs dealt him to Minnesota.

With the Yankees, Fontenot and teammate Ron Guidry—a fellow Cajun—would often converse in French.

Known as a methodical, fluid worker, Fontenot had an excellent sinker, a fair curve and a good slider.

He suffered one of the most embarrassing injuries in Cubs history. While serving as a reliever, Fontenot fell and bruised his ribs . . . when he tripped on his way to answer the bullpen telephone.

Augie Galan

A solid big league outfielder for 16 seasons, eight of them with the Cubs, Augie Galan once went an entire season without grounding into a double play.

A childhood injury nearly derailed Galan's dreams of playing in the majors, even after he'd proven himself at the highest strata of minor league baseball.

In 1935, Galan was the left fielder for Charlie Grimm's pennant-winning Cubs. Galan batted .314 and led the N.L. with 133 runs scored and 22 stolen bases. In 646 plate appearances, he didn't ground into a single double play . . . although he did hit into one triple killing.

Galan played the first 38 games of the 1936 season before hitting into a DP. The record still stands.

Before he joined the Cubs, the switch-hitting Californian was a star shortstop for the San Francisco Seals. Near the end of the 1932 season, the Seals let Galan leave the team with three games remaining so that he could join a barnstorming squad.

Galan's replacement at short? An 18-year-old local kid named Joe DiMaggio, who was also destined to make his mark as a big league outfielder.

Although Galan had proven himself in the fast-paced P.C.L., some big league scouts were skeptical. They'd heard about a childhood injury Galan had suffered. As a boy, he'd shattered his elbow and had never gone to a doctor. The arm didn't heal properly, and Galan had trouble making throws from the hole at short.

The Yankees wanted to purchase Galan's contract from San Francisco, and sent their top west coast scout to find out if he was damaged goods. Galan, who was unable to straighten his arm, took pains to conceal the deformity.

"I couldn't let anybody know," he said years later, "because it could have meant the end of my career."

The New York scout approached Galan and asked to see his arm. Galan refused, but the scout insisted. Knowing his chances with the Yanks were cooked, Galan decided not to bare his arm for the scout.

"Well, I was dead either way," he recalled, "so I decided not to remove my coat, and maybe it wouldn't get around and somebody else would take a chance on me."

The Cubs gambled on Galan, bringing him to Chicago in 1934.

Against the Dodgers on June 25, 1937, he became the first big leaguer to homer from both sides of the plate in the same game.

Galan batted .277 for the Cubs, and .287 lifetime. He tried to enlist during World War II, but was rejected because of his arm.

"There was almost no power in my right arm," Galan said. "Even batting left, the chips I had developed caused the arm to swell to twice its size. I had to freeze the elbow a half hour before every game. By the sixth or seventh inning, the feeling would come back, and if I had to make a throw it would be like somebody sticking needles in me."

Joe Girardi

Catcher Joe Girardi grew up in Peoria, Illinois, rooting for the Cubs. His favorite players were Ron Santo and Jose Cardenal.

As a 3rd grader, Girardi wrote a paper about wanting to play for the Cubs. He played baseball for Spalding Institute in Peoria, and for Northwestern University in Evanston, where he earned a degree in industrial engineering.

In 1986 Chicago took Girardi in the fifth round of the free-agent draft. Three years later, his boyhood dream came true when he joined the Cubs.

A member of the Yankees from 1996 to 1999, Girardi helped New York to three World Series titles.

After the '99 season he became a free agent and came back to the Cubs.

Mark Grace

Quick, now, what big league player had the most hits during the 1990s?

It wasn't Tony Gwynn, Wade Boggs, or Cal Ripken Jr. . . . but Mark Grace of the Cubs. Grace, Chicago's All-Star first baseman, recorded 1,754 hits from 1990 through 1999.

Grace's 364 doubles during that span is also the highest total of any major league player.

While Gwynn's approach is methodical—the Padres' batting star keeps an extensive video library and anticipates every pitcher's next delivery—Grace is a reactionary hitter who relies on instinct. "I just react to the ball," he says, ". . . see it, and hit it."

Gwynn and Grace are both products of San Diego State University. They frequently worked out together during their early days in baseball despite their philosophical differences.

S elected by the Cubs in the 24th round of the June 1985 draft, Grace didn't sign immediately. While holding out, he continued to play amateur ball. That summer, Grace's stock rose higher and higher and when he finally inked a Cubs pact—just in time for the 1986 season—he received a contract befitting a first-round choice.

In '86 Grace hit .342 for Peoria, becoming the first player to win the Midwest League batting title in his first year as a pro.

T wo years after he was drafted, Grace was challenging Leon Durham, the Cubs' incumbent first baseman. Already nicknamed "Amazing," Grace earned high praise from rival club officials.

"I take this job," said Don Zimmer, the new Cubs manager for 1988, "and I don't know Mark Grace. Then I go to the Winter Meetings, and I must have had at least two general managers from other organizations come to me and say, 'When Spring Training's over, Mark Grace will be your starting first baseman Opening Day.'"

S hortly after the first weeks of the exhibition season, it was obvious that Durham's days in Wrigley Field were numbered.

"After about three weeks of spring training, I could see what everybody was telling me," said Zimmer. "I could see that Mark Grace was a hell of a player."

The Cubs tried to deal Durham, but there were no takers. Grace was optioned to Iowa of the American Association before

Opening Day, and Durham started the season as Chicago's first baseman.

G race had batted .288 in the exhibition season, but the youngster took the demotion in stride.

"I knew from the start that as long as Leon was in Chicago, I'd be in Des Moines," Grace reflected. "But it's still a good situation for me here. I know I'm going to be playing every day and getting my at-bats. If I had stayed up there as a back-up player, I wouldn't be getting many at-bats. I'm only 23. I can be patient."

W hen Durham batted .219 after 24 games, the Cubs swapped him to Cincinnati and recalled Grace.

The rookie batted .296, earning N.L. Rookie of the Year honors from *The Sporting News.* Grace was the first Cub so honored since Kenny Hubbs in 1962.

Stan Hack and the
'45 Series

The Chicago Cubs won the 1938 N.L. pennant, capping off one of the most dramatic seasons in history. Pittsburgh had led the league since mid-July, but the Cubs kept nipping at their heels.

Bill Lee, Chicago's stalwart right-hander, won 22 games . . . including four straight shutouts in September to keep Chicago's hopes alive. With Pittsburgh up by half a game, the Cubs and Pirates squared off at Wrigley Field on September 28.

The score was 5-all in the bottom of the ninth with Mace Brown, Pittsburgh's ace reliever, on the mound. As darkness gathered, the umpires announced the game would be suspended at the end of the inning.

With two out and an 0-2 count, Chicago catcher Gabby Hartnett parked Brown's next pitch into the seats. Hartnett's "Homer in the Gloamin'" gave Chicago a half-game lead. A win over the Cardinals on October 1 gave them the pennant.

H artnett and Lee were two of the 1938 team's heroes, but the Cubs' most dependable hitter that year was Stan Hack.

A Cub since 1932 and the regular third baseman since 1934, Hack batted .320 and led the league in stolen bases in '38. In the World Series—a four-game sweep by the Yankees—the redoubtable Hack led the Cubs with a .471 average.

A line drive hitter, "Smilin' Stan" amassed 2,193 hits in 16 big league campaigns, all with Chicago.

He was also a sure-handed fielder who once played 54 consecutive games without an error.

" Stan Hack was a topnotch ballplayer his entire career," said outfielder Bill Nicholson, Hack's longtime roommate. "A good hitter, an adequate fielder. Not a great arm, but he got it over there in time. We were close, and ate our meals together a lot of the time."

Infielder Len Merullo says Hack's favorite post-game pastime was to "sit down and have a couple of bottles of beer and talk about the game."

"He was like Wade Boggs. He hit from foul line to foul line, a line drive type of hitter. Everybody loved Stan Hack. Stan was a very, very popular player."

Phil Cavarretta remembers Hack as "a happy-go-lucky man." He enjoyed life, enjoyed playing the game.

"Stan really was never given the credit he deserves. He could field bunts as well as anybody. And he was a good hitter . . . I can't understand why he isn't in the Hall of Fame."

After the 1943 season, the 34-year-old Hack called it quits. In 1944, with the Cubs pinched for players due to World War II, Hack staged a comeback.

In 1945 he had a career-best .323 batting average.

Hack sparked one of the most controversial calls in the '45 World Series. At Wrigley Field for Game Six with Detroit, with two out and the score tied 7-7 in the bottom of the 12th, Hack came to the plate with pinch runner Bill Schuster on first.

Hack sliced Dizzy Trout's next pitch into left field for what appeared to be an ordinary base hit. Detroit's Hank Greenberg charged in to field the ball, with the idea of holding Schuster at second.

But then, wrote veteran baseball reporter Fred Lieb, "to the amazement and joy of the crowd, the ball hopped over tall Hank's shoulder and rolled to the hedge."

Schuster scooted home with the winning run, sending the Series to a seventh game. Greenberg was charged with an error on Hack's hit.

Greenberg, a future Hall of Famer who had rejoined the Tigers that year after wartime service in the China-Burma-India Theater, was fuming—not only about the loss, but about the official scorers' decision.

"I never had a chance at the ball," Hank told reporters. "It was three feet over my head."

The ball, wrote Lieb, "had hit a hard spot, supposedly over a drain pipe, and . . . Greenberg had no earthly chance to field [it]."

At about 9 p.m. that night, the scoring board of Martin Haley, Ed Burns, and Harry Salsinger reconvened. They changed the call from a base hit and an error on Greenberg to a double for Hack.

It was the first time in Series history that a scorer's call had been reversed.

The Cubs lost the following day when the Tigers mauled Hank Borowy for five first-inning runs. Hack batted .367 in the '45 Series, giving him a lifetime average of .348 in four Fall Classics.

He retired for good after the 1947 season, and managed the Cubs from 1954 to 1956.

Ed Hanyzewski

Ed Hanyzewski, a Notre Dame alumnus, signed with Chicago prior to the 1942 season and earned a berth on the Cubs' opening day roster that year. Sent to the minors for seasoning, the right-hander rejoined the Cubs in 1943, going 8-7 with a 2.56 earned run average.

He remained with the Cubs through 1946, then retired to become a policeman in South Bend, Indiana. During the fall, Hanyzewski worked as a college football referee.

Ed's last name, pronounced "Hanna-zeski," gave Dizzy Dean fits when the former pitching great turned to broadcasting.

"I like to broke my jaw tryin' to pronounce that one," said Dean of his radio days in St. Louis. "But," he added, "I said his name by just holdin' my nose and sneezin'."

Billy Herman

G reatest Cubs second baseman ever?
Some say Ryne Sandberg, others claim it was Johnny Evers.
Many will argue for Billy Herman.

T here's no question, however, about the best number-two
hitter in Cubs history. Leo Durocher called Herman "an
absolute master at hitting behind the runner."

The Cubs starting second baseman from 1932 to 1943,
Herman batted .300 or better eight times in his 15-year stay in
the majors, including a .341 average in 1935.

" His first two years in the league," said Giants pitching great
Carl Hubbell, "he couldn't get a hit off me."

"So he set out methodically to figure me out. He did it. From 1933 on, I couldn't get him out."

Herman claimed he developed bat control because he was too light to pull the ball as a youngster.

"I learned to hit to right field early," he said, "because I only weighed about 150 pounds when I broke in. In those days, teams had maybe one or two power hitters and the rest of us had to move it around."

Herman was also a superb gloveman who once set an N.L. record for putouts in one season (466). With Billy Jurges, Herman formed one of the greatest Chicago double-play combinations.

He helped the Cubs to three pennants and played in 10 All-Star contests.

Herman, however, had a less-than-glorious major league debut. He joined the Cubs from Louisville of the American Association late in 1931, and got into his first game on August 28 against the Reds at Wrigley Field.

The rookie singled his first time up, but his second at-bat

was a disaster. Herman fouled off a pitch by Cincinnati's Si Johnson, and the ball struck him above the right ear. Herman had to be carried off the field.

The Cubs went on to win, 14-5, and Herman, who quickly recovered, went on to enjoy a great career.

For part of Herman's term in Chicago, Prohibition was the law of the land and Windy City gangsters grew wealthy and powerful off bootleg booze. Al Capone, Chicago's most feared mobster, liked baseball and was a frequent visitor to Wrigley Field.

"I saw him at the game many times," Herman recalled. "He was a Cubs fan.

"Those were tough days in Chicago."

Herman ended his playing days with Brooklyn and went on to manage the Pirates and Red Sox. In 1975 he was inducted into the Hall of Fame.

Tim Cohane summed up Herman's career in a 1947 magazine article: "He never was very fast. And he only had a fair arm. But he was brimful of batting and fielding talent, hustle, spirit and—most of all—brains.

"He was, as the players say, a professional."

Paul Hines

P aul Hines scored the first run in Cubs history.
It happened in Louisville on April 25, 1876, when Hines, batting cleanup and playing center field for the old White Stockings, raced home in the top of the second against the Grays for the first tally in a 4-0 Chicago victory.

B efore Al Spalding took over the managerial reins in Chicago for the National League's inaugural season in 1876, he evaluated each of his players. Hines, left fielder John Glenn and shortstop Johnny Peters were, in Spalding's opinion, the only "strong players on the Chicago nine."

Spalding imported three of his old teammates from Boston—catcher Deacon White, first baseman Cal McVey and second baseman Ross Barnes, plus Philadelphia's Adrian Anson and Ezra Sutton, a third baseman.

With this revamped squad, Chicago went 52-14. Hines led the team with 21 doubles and batted .331.

From Chicago, Hines moved on to the Providence Grays in 1878. According to baseball lore, he once guaranteed a home run—in writing.

Prior to a game at Boston, Hines allegedly went to the scorer's table and marked down a home run next to his name for the fifth inning.

Hines indeed came through with a homer in the designated frame, and the feat was widely publicized.

"It marked one of the few times in early baseball," wrote historian Lee Allen, "that the populace paid any attention to the home run, a department of play in which few fans appeared to be interested."

Hines is considered baseball's first Triple Crown winner, based on his 1878 season with Providence. He hit .358 with four homers and 50 RBI.

A year earlier, during the N.L.'s second season, league president William Hulbert publicly chastised Hines. In a letter published in a Chicago newspaper, Hulbert criticized his alleged indifference, poor attitude and poor play and warned the outfielder to "attend to your business" or be fined.

While Hines may have run afoul of the N.L. president, he was friendly with another chief executive: William McKinley, the 25th President of the United States.

Not long after Hines ended his professional baseball career in 1896, McKinley hired him as postmaster in the Department of Agriculture—a job Hines held for many years.

Rogers Hornsby

The acrimony between New York and Chicago during the 1932 World Series stemmed from the Cubs' split of the Series shares.

Before the Series began, the Chicago players had voted a half-share of Series swag to shortstop Mark Koenig. Koenig was a former Yank who'd joined the Cubs late in the year from San Francisco of the Pacific Coast League.

His .353 average in 33 games had helped the Cubs win the N.L. flag. Yankee players griped that the Cubs were cheapskates for not voting a full share to Koenig.

At least Koenig got something. Rogers Hornsby, who began the '32 season as Chicago's manager, didn't get a penny.

Many feel Hornsby was the game's greatest right-handed hitter of all time. Grover Alexander called the native Texan the toughest batter he ever faced.

Giving the argument plenty of heft is Hornsby's lifetime average of .358, plus three seasons above .400 (.401 in 1922, .424 in 1924, and .403 in 1925, for the Cardinals).

"As a hitter," said shortstop Woody English, Hornsby's infield partner and roommate, "Hornsby stood as far back in the right-hand corner of the batter's box as he could, and he stepped directly toward home plate. He stood right on the back line and strode right toward the front of that plate, and he'd hit the ball wherever it was pitched."

A second baseman, Hornsby spent three seasons and part of one other in Chicago.

In 1929, his last year as an everyday player, he batted .380—the highest average by a Cub in the Twentieth Century.

Hornsby managed the team from1930 through August 1932. On April 24, 1931, the Rajah—three days shy of his 35th birthday—put on a dazzling display. He hit three homers and drove in eight runs in a 10-6 road win over the Pirates.

Yet Hornsby was disliked by opponents and teammates alike. Abrasive, belligerent and crude, he berated his own players and feuded with his bosses.

"He was a very cold man," recalled Billy Herman. "He would stare at you with the coldest eyes I ever saw. If you did something wrong, he'd jump all over you.

"He was a perfectionist and had a very low tolerance for mistakes. He was one of the greatest hitters that ever lived— maybe the greatest—but he never talked hitting with us. He just expected you to go up there and do it."

H ornsby was a favorite of Cubs' owner Phil Wrigley. But Wrigley may have been Hornsby's only fan in the Chicago organization. Hornsby wouldn't allow reading, smoking, or drinking soda in the Chicago clubhouse.

"He didn't care about his players as people," claimed Dick Bartell, an N.L. shortstop from 1927 through 1946. Hornsby, said Bartell, was blunt with everyone, including team owners.

"Sam Breadon [who owned St. Louis] said that listening to Hornsby was like having the contents of a rock crusher emptied over his head," said Bartell.

B y August 1932 the Chicago brass was fed up, and Hornsby was dismissed following a widely-publicized argument with club president Bill Veeck Sr. The Cubs were 53-44 at the time. Charlie Grimm replaced the prickly Hornsby, and the Cubs went on to win the pennant.

"I put together a club that I thought would be capable of winning the pennant," said Hornsby. "We added [shortstop] Billy Jurges, Billy Herman, and [pitcher] Lon Warneke.

118

"Bill Veeck Sr., the president and general manager, tried to make some of my managing decisions from his office and it was obvious we didn't see eye to eye.

"We were in second place when I was fired, and it wasn't what Grimm did or didn't do that won the pennant for the Cubs. The first-place Pirates, the team to beat, lost 13 straight games."

" Most of the players were pretty happy about the change," recalled Billy Herman, "especially since it was Charley Grimm who took over. Grimm was as popular with the players as Hornsby was unpopular."

When the Cubs voted on Series shares, Hornsby didn't get a red cent.

"I didn't even get any share of the World Series money I was entitled to," grumbled Hornsby. "Not a penny."

Neither the Yankees nor anyone else in baseball uttered a peep in protest.

Kenny Hubbs

All his life, Kenny Hubbs was a winner. The California native pitched his Little League team to the championship game of the 1954 World Series in Williamsport, Pennsylvania.

On the way back home, 12-year-old Kenny and his dad stopped off at Wrigley Field for a Cubs' game, and saw Ernie Banks hit a pair of home runs.

In high school, Hubbs played shortstop on the baseball team and quarterbacked the football team. He also played basketball, high jumped for the track squad, and served as president of the senior class.

Although he was besieged with college scholarship offers, Kenny's mind was made up. He signed with the Cubs in the spring of 1959.

Late in 1961, Hubbs debuted in Chicago. A year later, he supplanted Don Zimmer as the Cubs' regular second baseman.

That June, Hubbs began an errorless streak that would stretch to a record 78 consecutive games. He handled 418 consecutive chances without a miscue, breaking the major league standard of 414 chances in 73 games set in 1948 by Bobby Doerr of the Red Sox.

"Kenny was built a lot like Ryne Sandberg," observed teammate Don Elston, a relief pitcher for the Cubs in 1953 and from 1957 to 1964. "He wouldn't have hit like Sandberg, but with that glove, there was nobody I've ever seen who was any better. He made the turn well and he was so smooth."

The 20-year-old Hubbs hit .260, won a Gold Glove award and was named N.L. Rookie of the Year.

It looked like the Cubs—an improving team with Hubbs and other flashy youngsters like 22-year-old third baseman Ron Santo and 23-year-old left fielder Billy Williams—were set at second base for years to come.

"He had great tools in the field," remembered Santo, "the best I've ever seen with Ryne Sandberg. He was graceful, talented, humble . . . it was clear from the very first he would make it immediately."

In his second full year with the Cubs, Hubbs' batting average dropped to .235 but his fielding was still close to perfection.

The Cubs improved to 82-80 in 1963, their first winning season since 1946.

Hubbs and Santo were roommates, and during the season the third baseman was surprised to learn that Hubbs planned to get a pilot's license. Hubbs had confided a fear of flying to Santo, and he hoped flying lessons would help him overcome the phobia.

On February 13, 1964, Hubbs was planning to fly a single-engine Cessna back to California from Provo, Utah, accompanied by Dennis Doyle, a lifelong pal. When the plane took off, there were snow flurries in the air and the temperature was below zero.

Moments after takeoff, the Cessna plunged into a frozen section of Utah Lake. Two days later, searchers recovered the bodies of Hubbs and Doyle.

Kenny Hubbs, who would have been the Cubs second baseman of the '60s—and perhaps one of the game's greatest of all time—died at the age of 23.

Hubbs' death set back the Cubs' development several years. Far worse, however, was the loss of one of finest men ever to don a Chicago uniform.

"He was a sparkplug who provided instant leadership and solidified our team," related Cubs pitcher Dick Ellsworth. With the arrival of youngsters like Hubbs, Santo, and Williams, Ellsworth figured the Cubs had the nucleus of a winning team.

"From the day he showed up, he was a great player and we knew he was going to be one of a kind," said Ellsworth. "We expected him to be our second baseman for at least a decade."

"To this day," says Ron Santo, "I still think about Kenny Hubbs and the kind of man he was. I miss him."

Randy Jackson

R andy Jackson's good looks earned the third baseman the nickname "Handsome Ransom".

Jackson broke in with Chicago in 1950 and played for the Dodgers and Indians before ending his career with the Cubs in 1959.

I n the second inning of a game at St. Louis on April 16, 1955, Jackson, Ernie Banks, and Dee Fondy hit consecutive home runs in a 7-5 loss to the Cardinals.

It was the second time in team history the Cubs had clouted back-to-back-to-back homers. On August 11, 1941, Phil Cavarretta, Stan Hack, and Bill Nicholson had consecutive homers in a 7-5 loss to the Cardinals at Sportsman's Park. The next time it happened, May 17, 1977, the Cubs finally won, destroying Pittsburgh 23-6 at Wrigley Field. In the fifth inning of the massacre, Larry Biittner, Jerry Morales, and Bobby Murcer hit three homers in a row.

Jackson played in the World Series (with the Dodgers in '56) and the All-Star Game, and also in the Cotton Bowl—for Texas Christian University in a 34-0 loss to Oklahoma State in 1945 and in 1946 for the University of Texas in a 40-27 win over Missouri.

"I wasn't any pro prospect," says Jackson. "I was an average football player that played a lot because we didn't have that many players. I didn't play football in high school, and went out in college for something to do."

Jackson's father had played baseball at Princeton. The elder Jackson had hopes for his son, but Randy didn't play any sports in high school.

It wasn't until he got to college that Jackson took up baseball and football. He led the Southwest Conference in hitting for three consecutive seasons.

Jackson was a two-time All-Star with the Cubs in 1954-1955.

The Dodgers obtained him as a possible successor to Jackie Robinson at third base, but a knee injury in 1957 shortened Jackson's career.

In the third inning of a game with the Phillies at Shibe Park on September 28, 1957, Jackson hit a three-run homer off Don Cardwell.

After the season the Dodgers moved to Los Angeles. Jackson's home run was destined to be the last by a Brooklyn player.

Fergie Jenkins

B ob Buhl and Larry Jackson.
  That's who the Cubs gave up to get Ferguson Jenkins from
the Phillies on April 21, 1966.

As part of the deal, the Cubs also obtained outfielder
Adolfo Phillips and first baseman John Herrnstein.

Buhl and Jackson had been reliable hurlers, but at the time
of the trade their best days were far behind them. They combined
for 47 wins and 53 losses in Philadelphia, and by the end of the
decade both were gone from the big leagues.

T he Cubs acquired Jenkins because Leo Durocher wanted to
  get rid of Ernie Banks.

Never a Banks fan during his stay in Chicago, Leo the Lip
hoped to pry loose Orlando Cepeda from San Francisco. When
the Giants instead dealt Cepeda to St. Louis, Durocher asked
Philadelphia about John Herrnstein, a promising first sacker.

The Cubs and Phils closed the deal, with Jenkins as an afterthought. Herrnstein played nine games for the Cubs and was traded to Atlanta less than six weeks later.

Banks stayed on first in Chicago, and Jenkins embarked on one of the great pitching careers in Cubs history.

The acquisition of Fergie Jenkins was one of the steals of the century. Jenkins, a 6' 5", 210-pound righty from Chatham, Ontario, was one of baseball's top control artists.

"What made Fergie so good was that he could locate a pitch anytime he wanted," says Ron Santo.

"He changed speeds better than anyone in the league. He didn't have the greatest fastball in baseball, but he could paint the outside corner."

His debut with the Cubs on April 23, 1966, foreshadowed great things to come.

In relief of starter Bob Hendley, Jenkins shut out the Dodgers for five and two-thirds innings. Jenkins also drove a pair of runs with a home run off Don Sutton in a 2-0 victory.

A good hitter, Fergie belted 13 career homers, including six in 1971.

O n an off-day during Spring Training in 1968, Jenkins went horseback riding with team captain Ron Santo, an experienced horseman, and teammates Glenn Beckert, Bill Hands, and Rich Nye. Jenkins' mount took off suddenly and made a sharp turn, sending the pitcher sprawling on the ground.

Santo was in a panic, figuring Jenkins was seriously hurt. When Santo rode over to his fallen teammate, the agonized Jenkins told him what had happened.

"I told him to stay," moaned Fergie, rubbing his leg. "But then he just took off on me. I thought I was under control because I was yelling 'Whoa!'"

"You can yell all you want," Santo exploded, "but unless you have the reins, it won't mean a darn thing!"

Santo and the others got Jenkins to a doctor, who advised the big hurler to stay off his feet for a week.

When Leo Durocher learned of the mishap, he threw a tantrum. Durocher was sure that Jenkins would be out for the beginning of the season. Yet 24 hours after the riding accident, Jenkins was back in uniform.

"Somehow, his Canadian blood had overcome the near disaster," recalls Santo. "Fergie did start for us Opening Day that year. He won 20 games for us. He didn't miss a start."

J enkins began putting up numbers unseen at Wrigley Field since Chicago's glory days prior to World War II. He was 20-13 in 1967, followed by seasons of 20-15, 21-15, 22-16, 24-13, and 20-12.

During those years he completed 140 of his 236 starts, hurled 24 shutouts and won the 1971 N.L. Cy Young Award. He was the bellwether of the Chicago squads of the late '60s and early '70s.

N one of this would've happened, however, if Jenkins had his way.

Jenkins thought he worked best in relief. Longtime Philadelphia star Robin Roberts saw Jenkins' true potential, however, and tried to convince the Phillies to convert the young pitcher into a starter.

But Phillies brass also considered Jenkins a relief pitcher and, with young left-hander Darold Knowles blossoming in the Philadelphia bullpen, Fergie was expendable.

I n the spring of '67, manager Leo Durocher and pitching coach Joe Becker convinced Jenkins to become a starting pitcher.

The switch gave the Cubs their most reliable right-handed starter since Three-Finger Brown.

" I think it was putting on the Cubs uniform that was always special to me," says Jenkins.

"I always tried to give the best performance I could, because the Cubs were the team that meant the most to me throughout my whole career."

Jenkins was inducted into the Hall of Fame in 1991.

Sam Jones

S am Jones had been a star pitcher in the Negro Leagues. He came to the Cubs in a trade with the Indians prior to the 1955 season. The right-hander had helped the Cleveland Buckeyes to the 1947 Negro Leagues World Series.

He signed with Cleveland in the wake of Jackie Robinson's ground-breaking debut with the Dodgers. With the Indians, however, Sam's path was blocked by a starting rotation that included future Hall of Famers Bob Feller, Bob Lemon, and Early Wynn, plus Mike Garcia.

T he right-handed Jones, who always chewed a toothpick on the mound, immediately became the bulwark of the Cubs pitching staff. His best pitch was a sweeping curve he'd learned from the legendary Satchel Paige.

Braves hurler Lew Burdette relates a story about Jones. Del Crandall, Milwaukee's good-hitting catcher, stepped up to the plate against Jones.

"Sad Sam threw him three curves," says Burdette, "and he fell down on each one and struck out. You couldn't help but laugh."

I n his first year in Chicago, Jones won 14 and lost 20 for a sixth-place team. He led the N.L. in strikeouts and walks, and he hurled four shutouts. Only Cincinnati's Joe Nuxhall, with five, had more.

"Sad Sam Jones was a nice, fun-loving guy," says Frankie Baumholtz, a Chicago outfielder from 1949 through 1955. "Despite his nickname, he always had a smile on his face. He always had a toothpick in his mouth, so they also called him 'Toothpick.'"

D uring that inaugural season with the Cubs, Jones was involved in one of the all-time great nail-biting games at Wrigley Field.

On May 12, 1955, he was pitching against the Pirates under overcast skies that held attendance to around 3,000. The Cubs scored in the first inning, and again in the second, fifth and sixth. They took a 4-0 lead into the top of the ninth and Jones, who'd walked four and fanned three through eight innings, hadn't allowed a hit.

Pittsburgh's lead off hitter, Gene Freese, bunted foul on the first pitch, then looked at four straight balls for a walk. Ex-Cub Preston Ward came up to bat for pitcher Vern Law. Ward worked the count to 2-2, and Freese made it to second on a wild pitch.

Jones then walked Ward, and Roman Mejias came in as a pinch runner.

When Jones walked rookie Tom Saffell on a 3-1 pitch to load the bases, manager Stan Hack asked for time and walked out to the mound. The Pirates had the tying run at the plate and Dick Groat, Roberto Clemente, and Frank Thomas—the heart of their order—due up.

Hack, who had two men warming up in the bullpen, called time and headed for the mound. "One more walk," Hack scolded Jones, "and I'm taking you out, no-hitter or not!"

"When I realized I was on the verge of blowing one of the better games I ever pitched," said Jones, "I told myself, 'They aren't going to get a hit now.' . . . I was going to get those last three outs . . . and that's all I thought about."

Sad Sam threw three straight curves to Groat for called strikes. Clemente lunged at a pair of curves and fouled off two pitches before swinging at a third strike. With a 1-2 count, Jones got Thomas looking for the final out—striking out three in a row after walking the bases loaded.

The no-hitter was the first in Wrigley Field since 1917, and the first in the big leagues by an African American pitcher.

In another bad trade, the Cubs dealt Jones to the Cardinals prior to the 1957 season. He went from St. Louis to San Francisco, and in 1959 his 21 victories tied for the N.L. lead.

Pitching for the Giants, Jones threw a second no-hitter, this time against the Braves in Milwaukee on April 28, 1961.

Sad Sam ended his big league career with the Orioles in 1964.

Whitey Lockman

Whitey Lockman, a 15-year outfielder-first baseman with the Giants, Cardinals, and Reds, managed the Cubs from 1972 through 1974.

Lockman took over for Leo Durocher and was succeeded by Jim Marshall. His slate at the Cubs helm was 157 wins and 162 losses.

His best work was in '72, after he replaced Durocher. The Cubs were 39-26 under Lockman and moved from fourth to second place.

Don Kessinger praised Lockman's leadership.

"If a ballplayer can't play for Whitey," said the Cubs shortstop, "he can't play for anybody."

Lockman was involved in a revolutionary event in 1973. On May 8 in San Diego, Lockman was ejected during a 12-inning 3-2 win over the Padres. With Lockman gone, Ernie Banks, by now a full-time Chicago coach, took over the managerial reins.

Technically, this made Mister Cub the first black manager in major league history. The incident took place two years before Frank Robinson was hired by the Cleveland Indians as the major league's first full-time African American field boss.

During Lockman's tenure, Cubs players lobbied to bring wives on the road. While the idea was under consideration, the Cubs dropped six of eight contests on a West Coast swing.

"Next trip," offered one wag, "the Cubs ought to bring the wives and leave the players home."

Dale Long

A rangy first baseman who played for six big league teams between 1951 and 1963, Dale Long hit eight home runs in eight consecutive games with Pittsburgh in May 1956.

Only one other player—the Yankees' Don Mattingly in 1987—has equaled that power display.

But the 6'4", 205-pound Long performed another unusual feat in 1958, this time as a Cub.

Scouted in high school by Casey Stengel, Long once passed up an offer to play for the National Football League's Green Bay Packers.

He debuted with the Pirates in 1951, and came to Chicago with outfielder Lee Walls in exchange for Gene Baker and Dee Fondy in May 1957. Ideally suited to the Friendly Confines, Long smashed 55 homers and batted .274 in two-plus seasons as a Cub.

During the first game of a double-header with the Pirates at Wrigley Field on August 20, 1958, skipper Bob Scheffing—himself an old Cubs catcher—inserted the left-handed Long behind the plate.

Years earlier, Pittsburgh general manager Branch Rickey had taken the unusual step of trying Long as a receiver. Long had even caught for one inning during a 1954 Pacific Coast League contest, when he played all nine positions for the Hollywood Stars.

Long took the field with chest protector, shinguards, his cap turned backwards, and—-since no lefty catchers gloves were available—his first baseman's mitt.

Long became the major leagues' first southpaw backstop in more than five decades.

On September 21 Long went behind the plate again, this time in the ninth inning of a home game with the Dodgers. How'd he do in his two-game big league catching career?

"Not bad," he boasted. "I picked a runner off first. Actually, I've never figured out any reason why a lefty couldn't play short or third, either."

Peanuts Lowrey

Harry "Peanuts" Lowrey, a child actor-turned baseball player, was an outfielder for the Cubs from 1942 through 1949.

Even after he made the majors, Lowrey continued to get bit parts in Hollywood.

Lowrey got into 27 games with the Cubs in 1942. A year later he replaced Dom Dallessandro as Chicago's center fielder.

Lowrey went off to war in 1944, but was back for the pennant-winning 1945 season. With Andy Pafko now in center, Peanuts shifted to left and batted .283.

He hit .310 against the Tigers in the World Series.

Charlie Grimm claimed Peanuts Lowrey was his son's favorite player. The boy followed Lowrey everywhere around the ballpark.

Grimm played first base while Lowrey manned left field for Chicago. Yet whenever anyone asked Charlie's son about his favorite Cub, his answer was always the same: Peanuts Lowrey.

"He didn't idolize me," lamented Jolly Cholly. "He idolized Peanuts."

Traded to Cincinnati in June 1949 as part of the deal that brought Hank Sauer to the Cubs, the 5'8", 170-pound Lowrey moved on to the Cardinals in 1950. He spent his final big league season with the Phillies in 1955.

Lowrey coached in the big leagues for 20 seasons, and was part of Leo Durocher's staff in 1969.

"The Cubs didn't blow it in '69," he insisted, "the darn Mets kept winning."

A native of Culver City, California, Lowrey stayed active in motion pictures during his playing days. He was an extra in *Pride of the Yankees* (1942), *The Stratton Story* (1949), and *The Winning Team* (1952), the film about Cubs' pitching great Grover Alexander.

Curiously, the credits for *The Winning Team* include quite a few past, present and future Cubs. Listed as a technical advisor is Jigger Statz, Alexander's Cubs teammate from 1922 to 1925.

Among the other extras are Lowrey, Hank Sauer, outfielders George Metkovich (who played briefly for Chicago in '53) and Irv Noren (1959-60), plus infielder Gene Mauch (a Cub in 1948-49).

T he script of the *The Winning Team* called for Lowrey to plunk Ronald Reagan in the head with a baseball. In one scene Reagan, playing Alexander, is forced at second base and Lowrey beans the future president with his throw to first on an attempted double play.

"I'm supposed to hit him in the head," Lowrey related. "Well, they got this two-by-four plank with a hole in it, and right behind that is the camera. I'm supposed to throw the ball right at this hole, which I do, and when it gets there they stop the cameras."

Lowrey said the ball that he threw at Reagan was actually made of cotton.

"He goes down and lies there," Lowrey continued. "I turn him over and I say, 'Sorry, Alex.' Then I'm supposed to look real soulful."

S o what was it like working with a future president?
"We'd have parties at night," Peanuts recalled, "and Reagan would come with his girl, Nancy Davis . . . They're married now. All of us thought he was a fine guy."

Bill Madlock

B ill Madlock grew up in Decatur, Illinois. He had around 150 college scholarship offers—for basketball.

Two schools, one in Trinidad, Colorado, the other in Keokuk, Iowa, offered him baseball scholarships.

I n 1970 Madlock signed his first professional contract with the Washington Senators. The franchise relocated to Texas in 1972 and Madlock joined the Rangers in 1973 after a 22-homer, .338 season at Spokane.

Cubs scout Gene Handley spotted Madlock at Spokane and was impressed by his compact swing. After the '73 season, the Cubs traded Fergie Jenkins to Texas for Madlock and infielder Vic Harris.

The original package was Madlock, Harris, and rookie catcher Jim Sundberg for Jenkins, catcher Randy Hundley, and outfielder Gene Hiser.

Cubs manager Whitey Lockman had second thoughts about the exchange, however, and wanted to sleep on it. A day later, the Rangers had cooled off on the deal.

The two teams finally reached an agreement and, in 1974, Madlock supplanted Ron Santo at third base in Wrigley Field.

Madlock's .313 was the highest average by a Cub third baseman since Stan Hack's .323 in 1945. He won back-to-back N.L. bat titles in 1975-1976.

Was Madlock a natural hitter?

"I didn't have this knack for going to all fields until I hit the major leagues," he claims. "In my last year of Triple-A ball, I considered myself a pull hitter . . . but when I got up here and saw how these guys pitch, I shortened my stroke and started going to all fields."

Madlock claims he wielded a potent bat as a youngster.

"In Little League I hit .700 or .800," he recollects. "Then in my last year in high school, in American Legion ball, I hit about .430."

Was it coaching?

"No, man . . . you know how it is in Legion ball. The coach is usually your mailman or something and they usually only get there in time for the games. I just worked on hitting by myself."

The Cubs dealt Madlock to San Francisco after the 1976 season. He also played for the Pirates and Dodgers, retiring after the 1987 season with a career .305 batting average.

He hit .336 in an even 400 games as a Cub.

Ed Mayer

Left-hander Ed Mayer pitched in 22 games for the Cubs in 1957 and 1958, splitting four decisions.

One of the bespectacled Mayer's victories was a win over Dodger great Sandy Koufax.

On May 30, 1958, the Cubs took two games from Los Angeles at Wrigley Field, winning 3-2 and 10-8. In the second game, Mayer and Koufax both came on in relief. The Cubs touched the future Hall of Famer for two runs in the bottom of the ninth for the victory.

The win was Mayer's last. Chicago farmed him out to the Pacific Coast League in June. He bounced around until 1959, but never returned to the majors.

Those two stints with the Cubs remain one of the highlights of Mayer's life.

"When I put on that Cub uniform and walked on the diamond at Wrigley Field, that was the biggest thrill of my life," he says. "They often make fun of the Cubs. But from my point of view, it was great being a Cub. It was a beautiful park, wonderful fans, great city."

The personalized license on Mayer's car reads "OLD CUB".

LindyMcDaniel

F rom 1955 through 1975, forkball specialist Lindy McDaniel pitched for the Cardinals, Cubs, Giants, Yankees, and Royals.

McDaniel joined the Cubs in 1963, replacing Don Elston as the bullpen stopper. In three full seasons with Chicago, he saved 39 games.

A control pitcher, McDaniel didn't have a great fastball but was adept at working out of a jam. His forte was the forkball, a pitch McDaniel learned from Pirate reliever Roy Face.

D uring a 1963 game against the Giants, McDaniel looked like Cy Young and Babe Ruth rolled into one.

At Wrigley Field on June 6, 1963, the Cubs and Giants were tied at 2-2 in the top of the 12th. With one out, the Giants loaded the bases against Barney Schultz, and Chicago skipper Bob Kennedy summoned McDaniel from the bullpen.

The right-hander promptly picked off Willie Mays at second base, and then quashed the San Francisco rally by striking out Ed Bailey.

McDaniel wasn't done yet. In the bottom of the inning, he stepped up against southpaw Billy Pierce. On a 2-2 count, McDaniel slammed Pierce's next delivery into the left field stands for a 3-2 Cubs win.

The triumph was the Cubs' 11th in 13 games and put them in a three-way tie for first place with St. Louis and San Francisco.

It marked the first time Chicago stood atop the league since May 1958.

Bill Nicholson and
Wartime Baseball

Wartime Player.

That label hung like a cloud over many of baseball best players 1942 through 1945. The United States entered World War II in December 1941. When big league players entered military service, their places on the rosters were filled by minor leaguers. When those men were drafted, players from further down the depths of the minors took their place.

With Ted Williams in the Marine Corps, Bob Johnson—a solid major leaguer in his day, but by then 38 years old and past his prime—patrolled left field for the Red Sox.

While Pee Wee Reese was in the navy, Eddie Basinksi took over as Brooklyn's shortstop.

At Yankee Stadium, Tuck Stainback became New York's center fielder after Joe DiMaggio went off to war.

When peace returned in 1945, so did Williams, Reese, DiMaggio and the rest of the stars. Many of the players who filled during their absence quietly drifted back into obscurity.

A t one time or another during the war years, 27 Cubs traded baseball flannels for military uniforms. They were:
    • *Pitchers:* Dale Alderson, Hi Bithorn, Bill Fleming, Emil Kush, Walt Lanfranconi, Red Lynn, Russ Meers, Vern Olsen, Johnny Schmitz, Lon Warneke.
    • *Catchers:* Marv Felderman, Mickey Livingston, Clyde McCullough, Bob Scheffing, Joe Stephenson, Bennie Warren.
    • *Infielders:* Cy Block, Al Glossop, Lou Stringer, Bob Sturgeon, Eddie Waitkus.
    • *Outfielders:* Dom Dallessandro, Charlie Gilbert, Peanuts Lowrey, Lou Novikoff, Whitey Platt, Marv Rickert.

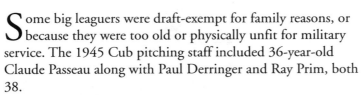

S ome big leaguers were draft-exempt for family reasons, or because they were too old or physically unfit for military service. The 1945 Cub pitching staff included 36-year-old Claude Passeau along with Paul Derringer and Ray Prim, both 38.
    Forty-three-year-old Johnny Moore, a Chicago outfielder in the late '20s and early '30s who hadn't played in the majors since 1937, was pressed into service for seven games during the '45 campaign.

S ometimes players who were too young for military service donned major league uniforms. During the 1944 season, Joe Nuxhall of the Cincinnati Reds pitched in his first game as a 15-year-old.

Players like pitcher Hal Newhouser of Detroit and Yankee second baseman Snuffy Stirnweiss, who came into their own during the war years, are sometimes dismissed as Wartime Players—men who excelled against watered-down competition.

That "Wartime Player" tag early kept Newhouser (who won 207 games between 1939 and 1955) out of the Hall of Fame.

Despite the vagaries of wartime baseball, the Cubs waged a tight battle with the St. Louis Cardinals for the 1945 N.L. title.

"That wasn't an easy season," maintains Phil Cavarretta. "Even though it was during the war, there were a lot of good players still around, and more were coming home from the war."

Some critics dismiss Bill "Swish" Nicholson, the Cubs' power-hitting right fielder of the 1940s, as a Wartime Player. A refugee from Connie Mack's Athletics (Nicholson was 0-for-12 for Philadelphia in 1936), Nicholson refined his talents at Chattanooga under the tutelage of Lookouts' manager Kiki Cuyler, an ex-Cub.

Nicholson developed into one of the Southern League's most feared sluggers and in June 1939—tipped off by Cuyler—the Cubs purchased Nicholson's contract.

It was the fans in Brooklyn—the same folks who dubbed Cardinals great Stan Musial "Stan the Man"—who gave Nicholson the nickname "Swish."

Every time the muscular ex-dairy farmer cut loose with a powerful practice swing, the awed Flatbush crowds would respond with a respectful cry of "Swish!"

It was the crosstown rival Giants, however, who accorded Nicholson the greatest show of deference. With the Cubs trailing in the seventh inning of a July 23, 1944, contest, New York manager Mel Ott ordered his pitcher, Andy Hansen, to walk Nicholson with the bases loaded.

Nicholson had been on a rampage, hitting four consecutive homers over two games. In a 40-hour span he'd clubbed a total of six round-trippers. Ott wasn't taking any chances, and took the bat right out of Nicholson's hands—even if it cost him a run.

The strategy worked. The base on balls to Nicholson forced in a run, but the Giants went on to win, 12-10.

Nicholson also received a compliment from an army paratrooper. Just before he went overseas, the serviceman sent the Chicago outfielder a letter.

"I've always admired your playing," wrote the soldier, "and I wonder if you'd be so kind as to send me a Cubs cap. I'd like to wear it into battle."

Nicholson made sure the G.I. got his cap.

Prior to Pearl Harbor in 1940 and '41, Nicholson had chalked up impressive 25- and 26-homer seasons. He belted 29 home runs with 128 RBI in 1943, followed by a 33-homer, 122 RBI campaign in 1944.

Nicholson lost the '44 N.L. MVP award to St. Louis Cardinals shortstop Marty Marion by a single vote.

Swish was also a capable fielder with a decent throwing arm. He was also a smart base runner, as future Hall of Fame second baseman Red Schoendienst found out the day he made his major league debut.

On Opening Day in 1945, Nicholson scored the winning run in the bottom of the ninth on a single by Don Johnson. Nicholson beat the throw home by the rookie Schoendienst, who was playing left field.

Oddly, Nicholson batted only .243 for the pennant-winning Cubs in 1945, with 13 homers. During the off-season, he worked at a Maryland defense plant. He underwent an army physical exam in '45, but was never called for military duty.

Nicholson would later recall that during the '45 season he "felt bad all the time. No pep." He still managed to drive in eight runs in the World Series, won by Detroit in seven games.

Five years later, when he played for the Phillies, doctors discovered Bill's problem. He was a diabetic, and the ailment prevented him from playing in the 1950 Series with the Yankees.

The '45 Series was Bill's last, just as it was for the Cubs—at least in the Twentieth Century.

Swish Nicholson, downgraded by some as a Wartime Player, ranks among the Cubs' all-time leaders in a half-dozen offensive categories.

Lou Novikoff

Lou Novikoff was a four-time minor league batting champ who played for the Cubs from 1941 to 1944. Born in Arizona, Novikoff spoke nothing but Russian until he was about 10.

Dubbed "The Mad Russian," Lou was proud of his ethnic heritage and owned a Russian wolfhound. He once broke out of a slump after his wife fed him Russian-style ground beef rolled in cabbage leaves and served on a bun.

Novikoff was a notoriously bad outfielder. He blamed some of his defensive problems on Wrigley Field's ivy-covered walls, believing the foliage was actually poison ivy.

Novikoff also claimed he had trouble playing left field at Wrigley because the foul lines were crooked.

After the Cubs shipped him to the minor leagues, Lou complained that the outfield in Milwaukee (then part of the American Association) had too many bumps.

After retiring from baseball, Novikoff was elected to the Hall of Fame . . . not the baseball shrine in Cooperstown, but the Softball Hall of Fame in Rockford, Illinois.

Softball was actually Novikoff's first love. He once struck out 22 batters in an eight-inning game, and played until he was 53 years old.

Milt Pappas

Right-hander Milt Pappas won 209 big league contests between 1957 and 1973 for the Orioles, Reds, Braves, and Cubs.

He started the 1965 All-Star contest for the A.L., and after the season was part of one of the most controversial trades in history. Pappas went to the Reds in a four-player deal that brought Frank Robinson to Baltimore.

Robinson proceeded to win the 1966 A.L. MVP Award, sparking the Orioles to a four-game World Series sweep of the Dodgers.

In 1970 Pappas, by then 31 years old, joined the Cubs from Atlanta.

The Detroit native was 51-41 in three-plus seasons in Chicago, winning a career-high 17 games in 1971 and '72.

B y 1972 the Cubs were starting to slip. Leo Durocher quit as manager in late July, handing over the club to director of player development Whitey Lockman. The Cubs revived, at least temporarily, and finished second, 11 games behind Pittsburgh in the N.L. East.

In 1973 the Cubs finished under .500 for the first time in seven seasons. They wouldn't be winners again until 1984.

But one afternoon in '72, Pappas gave Chicago fans something they'd never forget when he came within one pitch of a perfect game.

O n September 2 at Wrigley Field, Pappas took the mound against the Padres. The Cubs gave him plenty of support, scoring two runs in the first, another pair in the third and four more in the eighth.

Meanwhile, Pappas' slider was unhittable. Heading into the last inning, he'd retired 24 Padres in a row.

John Jeter led off the ninth for San Diego and hit a short fly into center. Center fielder Billy North broke back, lost the ball in the sun, and then fell. As the crowd gasped and Pappas' heart sunk to his toeplate, Billy Williams came streaking over from left field to make a fine running catch. Fred Kendall, the next batter, grounded out to shortstop Don Kessinger.

With the pitcher due up, San Diego skipper Don Zimmer called on Larry Stahl, a .226 hitter. Stahl swung and missed the first pitch. Pappas' next delivery was wide. Stahl missed again on the next pitch, and the Wrigley Field fans were on their feet. No Cubs pitcher had ever thrown a perfect game.

Pappas' next two pitches were close but, said home plate ump Bruce Froemming, both were outside. With a full count, Pappas delivered. Stahl watched.

From third base, Ron Santo saw what looked "like a knee high strike" for what he thought was the third out.

Yet Froemming barked "Ball four!" and Stahl became the first San Diego baserunner. Pappas had missed perfection by inches. It was a heartbreaking moment for Milt, for the Cubs and for the crowd of nearly 13,000 on hand that day.

Moments later, Pappas salvaged a no-hitter when he retired ex-Cub Garry Jestadt on a pop-up caught by second baseman Carmen Fanzone.

Afterward, Cubs catcher Randy Hundley mused on how close Pappas had come to pitching a perfect game.

"They were so close," said Hundley, "I don't know how Stahl could take them."

Pappas shook off the near miss.

"I always said I'd rather be lucky than good," he philosophized, "and today I was lucky."

Pappas' performance delighted manager Whitey Lockman.

"I've been in professional baseball thirty years," he enthused, "and this is the first time I've been on the winning side of a no-hitter. I couldn't believe the thrill."

The day of his no-hitter, Pappas almost called in sick.

The 1972 season had been a tough one for Milt. He'd broken a finger during Spring Training. His elbow had given him trouble throughout the season, requiring repeated cortisone shots. Early in the season he'd missed a few starts with a bad back.

In early September, he was suffering from a bad cold. Feeling miserable, Pappas was ready to call the ballpark to say he wouldn't be coming to work. But his wife, Caroline, convinced him to give it a try.

The Padres were sorry she did.

P appas had a near-miss in one other category.

During his 17-year career, he won 209 games. Ninety-nine of those wins were in the N.L.

Just one more would have made Pappas one of a handful of pitchers with a 100 victories in both leagues.

Bob Ramazzotti

Infielder Bob Ramazzotti spent all or part of seven seasons in the major leagues, including a hitch with the Cubs from 1949 to 1953.

To Randy Jackson, "Ram" was the Roommate From Hell.

A 5'8½", 175-pounder from Pennsylvania, Ramazzotti was a former Dodger whose pro career started in 1940. After missing 1942 through 1945 due to military service, he spent all of 1946 with Brooklyn as a backup at third and short.

In May 1949 the Dodgers sent him to Chicago for infielder Hank Schenz. For a stretch in 1951, Ramazzotti took over at shortstop after a broken leg shelved Roy Smalley.

The following year, Ram played 50 games at second and batted .284 despite spending time on the disabled list. A hand injury limited Ramazzotti to 39 at-bats in '53, his last year in the majors. He batted .230 lifetime, including .236 for Chicago.

Randy Jackson, the Cubs' third baseman during the early '50s, roomed briefly with Ramazzotti during road trips and couldn't wait to get away from him.

"He was a wonderful guy," Jackson recollects, "but he smoked Italian cigars that just curled your hair. I didn't smoke, so I told him he'd have to get someone else."

Charlie Root and Babe's "Called Shot"

The great Babe Ruth hit 714 home runs during his career, and 15 more in 10 World Series. None was more controversial than Ruth's home run off Chicago right-hander Charlie Root in Game Three of the 1932 Fall Classic at Wrigley Field.

Baseball legend says that Ruth strode toward the plate with one out in the fifth inning, the jeers and taunts of the multitude floating down like spent shrapnel. There was bad blood between the Cubs and Yanks in that World Series and, according to myth, the only people not booing the Bambino that day were Ruth's Yankee teammates and the umpires.

The score was 4-all with the Yanks leading the Series, two games to none. Ruth had knocked a three-run homer in the first off Root, and nearly 50,000 Cubs fans were all over the Bambino like Sammy Sosa on a hanging curve.

Even baseball commissioner Kenesaw Mountain Landis, himself fluent in barbaric dialect, was taken aback by the language.

From there, fact and fantasy blend. Even film doesn't prove or disclaim what happened next. On a 1-2 count, Ruth swung and connected. The ball sailed straight out toward the flagpole in center field and sank into the bleachers. Ruth had homered into the deepest regions of Wrigley Field.

But had Ruth called his shot?

A few reporters, most notably John Drebinger of the *New York Times,* wrote that Babe had pointed to the exact spot where he hit his home run.

Most other scribes, however, made no mention of such an incident. Even Ruth's biographer, Robert Creamer, cast doubts upon the veracity of the "Called Shot."

No way, said the Chicago players.

Had Ruth pulled a stunt like that, they insisted, Charlie Root—remembered by one contemporary as "one of the roughest, toughest competitors who ever lived" and a "hard-nosed, hard-assed pitcher"—would have tried to stick the next pitch in the Babe's ear for grandstanding.

The stocky Root is the winningest pitcher in Cub history, with 201 career victories. He helped Chicago win four pennants, and was still pitching in the major leagues at age 42.

When he left the Cubs after the 1941 season, Root returned to the minors and kept on pitching until he was 49.

Years later, a long-forgotten homemade film of the episode surfaced. In it, Ruth appears to make some kind of gesture with his hands.

But was he pointing to a spot in center field? Several Yankee players swore he did, and the Babe—ever the showman—always milked the story without giving a straight answer.

Was Charlie Root someone the Bambino would try to show up?

"Root would have murdered him," claimed Chicago infielder Woody English.

"He [Ruth] didn't point," insisted second baseman Billy Herman. "Root would have had him with his feet up in the air."

"I'd have knocked him on his fanny," growled Root.

But the legend of the Called Shot has transcended myth and hardened, for many, into fact. As longtime *Washington Post* sportswriter Shirley Povich noted, "Who could ever forget the scene, even if he never saw it?"

P erhaps Cubs catcher Gabby Hartnett offered the most logical explanation. Hartnett maintains that after Root got two strikes on the Babe, Ruth held up a finger toward the jeering Cub dugout and said, "It only takes one to hit it."

No matter what, Ruth's homer signaled the Cubs' downfall. Lou Gehrig followed with another home run, and the Yanks went on to win, 7-5. The Yanks won again the following day to complete the sweep.

A ll but forgotten amid the controversy over the Called Shot is the fact that Root surrendered Babe Ruth's last home run in World Series play.

Vic Saier and Mrs. O'Leary's Cow

Wrigley Field, the home of the Cubs, opened in 1914 as Weeghman Park. Restaurateur Charles Weeghman built the ballpark at Clark and Addison for his Chicago Whales club of the Federal League.

Weeghman purchased the Cubs after the Federal League's demise. He uprooted the team from the West Side Grounds at Polk and Lincoln (now Wolcott), the Cubs' home park since 1893, and brought them to the park that bore his name.

Prior to the formation of the National League in 1871, Chicago had a team in the National Association, an early professional circuit.

The thriving city was proud of its ballclub, and an area beside Lake Michigan was set aside for the team's new home at Randolph, Michigan, and Madison Streets. Known as Lake Park, the ballfield was closer to the water in those days (over the

years, the shoreline has been extended further eastward via landfill projects).

In October 1871, Mrs. O'Leary's cow allegedly started the fire that consumed 2,600 city acres. Lake Park was destroyed by the conflagration. Without a place to play, the Windy City's baseball team disbanded.

Professional baseball didn't return to Chicago until 1874.

Chicago's N.L. franchise called several locations home, including the 23rd Street Grounds (23rd and State, 1876-1877); Lakefront Park (south of Randolph Street between Michigan Avenue and Illinois Central railroad tracks, 1878-1884); West Side Park (Congress and Throop Streets, 1885-1892); and the West Side Grounds (1893-1915).

The Cubs's first game in the new park took place April 20, 1916.

Vic Saier, who had taken over at first base from Frank Chance after the 1911 campaign, was the hero in that contest. The 24-year-old Michigander hit a sacrifice fly in the bottom of the 11th, driving in the winning run in the Cubs' 7-6 triumph over Cincinnati.

A Cub from 1911 to 1917, Saier's career was curtailed by a back injury. The lifetime .263 hitter finished up with Pittsburgh in 1919.

Saier, whose 21 triples topped the N.L. in 1913, has one other distinction: his five career home runs against Christy Mathewson (including four in 1914) are the most off the Hall of Fame pitcher.

Ryne Sandberg

For several years, two of Chicago's greatest sportsmen wore number 23: Michael Jordan of the Bulls and the Cubs' Ryne Sandberg.

Both retired at a young age, both made brief comebacks and then quit for good, at an age when many of their contemporaries were still playing every day.

Like Michael Jordan, Sandberg was an all-out competitor. When Jordan, observed Sandberg, decided he was "mentally tired out getting to that level [of intensity] every time out, he walked away." And, added Ryne, "in that sense, so did I."

What a legacy Sandberg left behind! What Billy Herman was to Chicago in the first half of the century, Sandberg was to the latter-day Cubs: a brilliant second baseman who could do

it all. His .285 lifetime batting average and 282 homers tell only half the story.

Sandberg was one of the all-time great fielders at second base. He once played 123 consecutive games without an error, and he shares the big league record for the highest fielding percentage by a second baseman (.989).

S andberg, a native of Spokane, Washington, came to the Cubs from the Phillies in January 1982 along with Larry Bowa for Ivan DeJesus.

It's hard to believe now but, when Ryne came to Chicago he was a man without a position. Sandberg had signed with Philadelphia as a shortstop and had also played third and second in the minors.

The Cubs had Bowa at short, Ken Reitz at third, and Bump Wills at second. During his first Spring Training with the Cubs, Sandberg spent time at each of those positions, and in center field as well. "I had three different gloves in my locker," he recalled, "and I didn't know what to think."

T oward the end of spring camp, manager Lee Elia gave Sandberg the word: Reitz was going to be released, and Sandberg was now the Cubs' third baseman.

Ryne responded with a .271 average. He fielded beyond expectations, making just 11 errors all year.

In September, however, general manager Dallas Green abruptly informed Sandberg he was moving to second base.

Sandberg took a crash course on how to play second base from an unlikely tutor: Cubs pitching coach Billy Connors. Despite his job description and portly build, Connors proved to be a capable teacher.

"He showed me, with that bad body of his, how to turn the double play and then jump afterward," says Sandberg.

Sandberg's biggest problem was trying to hold a straight face every time Connors tried to turn a pivot in less-than-balletic movement.

While Connors didn't look like the ideal infield instructor, he turned out to be an excellent teacher. Just a few days after the fielding lesson, Pete Rose of the Phillies observed Sandberg's work around the bag and predicted Sandberg would be an All-Star at second base.

Sandberg turned out to be even better than that, earning the N.L. MVP in 1984. That year he batted .314 with 200 hits, including 36 doubles, 19 triples, 19 home runs, and 32 stolen bases. He barely missed becoming the first big leaguer to collect 200 hits, 20 doubles, 20 triples, 20 homers, and 20 stolen bases.

Until 1984, Sandberg saw himself as a singles hitter. It was Jim Frey, who managed the Cubs from 1984 to 1986, who convinced him he could be a power hitter.

"I just thought he had too much talent not to take advantage of it, too much talent to remain a line-drive hitter," says Frey, who claims he had no quarrel with Ryne's hitting style.

Frey just wanted Sandberg to know that he had the

potential, at 6'2" and with ample body strength, to be a line drive hitter with power.

"I wasn't trying to make him a home run hitter," insists Frey. "What I told him was that on certain pitches I knew he could handle, he should be looking to drive the ball for extra bases, instead of just settling for singles."

Sandberg listened to Frey's suggestion, and doubled his extra-base hit production from 37 in 1983 to 74 in 1984.

During the summer of 1969, the year Sandberg celebrated his 10th birthday, he would head for Fairgrounds Park in his native Spokane to watch the local Indians of the Pacific Coast League. Spokane was the Triple-A affiliate of the Dodgers, and 19-year-old Bill Buckner was a highly-regarded outfielder-first baseman.

Thirteen years later, following the trade with the Phillies, Sandberg and Buckner became teammates.

"I never let Buckner forget that I used to watch him play when I was a kid," chortles Sandberg.

In 1970, Sandberg began following the career of Larry Bowa, then a rookie shortstop with the Phillies. The youthful Sandberg idolized Bowa, and became his teammate when he joined Philadelphia in 1981.

Bowa was traded to Chicago with Sandberg prior to the 1982 season. Playing third for the Cubs that season, Sandberg found himself in the same infield with two of his boyhood heroes: Buckner on first and Bowa at short.

Sandberg's first year with the Cubs started out like a nightmare. The youngster had just one hit in his first 32 at-bats. He hung in there, however, and finished at .271.

Throughout Sandberg's ordeal, Bowa never lost faith in his infield partner. The veteran kept telling the other Cubs that Sandberg would be able to do everything that Mike Schmidt could do, except hit with Schmidt's awesome power.

Sandberg's toughness in the face of his early-season adversity really impressed Bowa.

"No knock on Schmitty," Bowa said, "but he might have panicked if he'd gone though anything like that as a rookie. Ryne Sandberg never came close to panicking."

Derwent Sandberg, Ryne's father, was a real baseball fan. Ryne claims he was named after Ryne Duren, a hard-throwing Yankee relief pitcher in the late 1950s and early '60s.

"My dad had taken my mother to . . . see the Yankees play when she was pregnant with me," says Sandberg, ". . . and the name just stuck."

According to Sandberg, his brother Del was named for former big league outfielder Del Ennis.

"Yeah," Sandberg says with a grin, "my dad was quite a baseball fan."

Ron Santo and the '69 Cubs

During an era of excellent third basemen—Brooks Robinson of Baltimore, the Braves' Eddie Mathews, Frank Malzone of Boston, the Cardinals' Ken Boyer and his brother, Clete Boyer of the Yankees—Ron Santo stood out.

Even Cubs skipper Leo Durocher, with whom Ron had a stormy relationship during their seven years together in Chicago, praised Santo.

"When I took over the club," said Durocher, "I looked upon Santo as one of my greatest assets. He was the best-fielding third baseman in the National League, and he knocked in his 100 to 110 runs a year."

A Cub from 1960 through 1973, Santo ended his playing days with the White Sox in 1974. He batted .277 with 342 homers and was an excellent glove man who set several fielding records.

When his career ended, the fiery Seattle native became a Cubs color commentator on WGN. Like Ernie Banks, Santo is as much a part of the Windy City as the Sears Tower or deep-dish, thick-crust pizza.

Yet he came close to playing for the Dodgers early in his career.

During the 1961 season, Santo's second in the majors, the Cubs were playing Los Angeles. The Dodgers' third base coach was Leo Durocher, who would become Santo's manager in Chicago four years later.

Just before the game, Durocher told Santo he was headed for stardom.

"By the way," added Leo, "you might be wearing a Dodger uniform tomorrow."

Trade rumors began to swirl. Word was that L.A. wanted Santo badly. Third base had been a revolving door for the Dodgers since Billy Cox's departure after the 1953 season.

According to the scuttlebutt, Los Angeles would give up pitcher Stan Williams, outfielder-first baseman Ron Fairly, and power-hitting outfielder Frank Howard for Santo.

Fortunately for Chicago fans, the trade never took place. The Dodgers won pennants in 1963 (platooning veteran Jim Gilliam at third with rookie Ken McMullen) and '66 (with Gilliam and John Kennedy sharing the hot corner).

The Cubs' best finish in the ensuing years was second in the N.L. East in 1969.

A ny regrets? No way, insists Santo.
"There's no place you can go in the United States," he says, "any city or team, where, if you lose, they still get the support the people give you here. The fans here are the best."

C ubs fans' loyalty was severely tested in '69 when the Mets overtook the Cubs for the Eastern Division title and went on to win the N.L. pennant at the World Series. Over the years, the Cubs' '69 collapse has sparked more theories than an Oliver Stone film.

- Durocher didn't provide the right leadership and twice went AWOL from the team.
- The Cubs quit hitting down the stretch.
- Durocher wore out his regulars.
- The Cubs didn't have enough bench strength.
- Durocher's hostile approach toward his own players backfired.
- The Cub players were too concerned with off-field enterprises.
- Et cetera, et cetera, et cetera . . .

The fact is, the Mets outplayed the Cubs down the stretch.

Some claim the summer of '69 produced two miracles: the lunar landing and the Mets winning the N.L. pennant.

Nonsense. The Apollo expedition and the '69 Mets were both the end product of diligent preparation, execution and leadership. The man who provided the Mets' leadership was Gil Hodges.

"The New York Mets were the worst team in the league," wrote outfielder Curt Flood in his autobiography.

"When some of the youngsters showed signs of becoming first-rate professionals, Gil Hodges was named manager and they became serious."

The '69 Mets were a terrific team.

So were the '69 Cubs.

Did Bobby Thomson's homer make the 1951 Dodgers any less of a great ballclub? Chicago's lineup of Randy Hundley, Ernie Banks, Don Beckert, Don Kessinger, Santo, Billy Williams, and Jim Hickman was one of the most potent in history.

Fergie Jenkins, Ken Holtzman, Bill Hands and Phil Regan could command millions of dollars today on the free-agent market.

But the Mets won, and that's baseball.

The real tragedy is that Ron Santo nor Gil Hodges—two central figures in that great '69 season—have been repeatedly ignored in Hall of Fame balloting.

hat made Santo's achievements all the more incredible is the debilitating ailment that dogged him throughout his career.

Honored in ceremonies at Wrigley Field during August 1971, Santo revealed that he was a lifelong diabetic. He made arrangements for all proceeds from Ron Santo Day to be donated to the Diabetes Association of Chicago.

S anto wasn't immune to an occasional mental lapse. During the 1969 season, Dick Selma approached him with a trick play. With two out and a full count on a good hitter and runners on first and second moving with the pitch, Selma said he would go into the stretch, take his foot off the rubber, and then lob the ball to Santo at third.

The move was technically a balk, but Selma figured he might be able to catch the umpires off guard and nail the runner going into third. If he didn't, reasoned Selma, the runners would move up on the balk call, and Selma could then dispose of the good hitter at the plate by putting him on first base by throwing a ball on the next pitch.

Selma and Santo agreed on a signal. If the Cubs found themselves in the right circumstances, Selma would look at Santo and yell, "Two out! Knock it down!"

This disingenuous comment, of course, is basic baseball strategy: guard the line with a runner in scoring position; let nothing hit to the corners get through for extra bases.

Santo and Selma came up with Santo's countersign, which would be a simple "Yeah!" With that, Santo would creep toward the baseline to be ready for Selma's throw.

One night in September, Selma ran the count to 3-2 on Philadelphia's Dick Allen with two out and runners on first and second. Selma looked over at the intense Santo, who was guarding the line.

"Two out, knock it down," yelled Selma, waiting for the countersign.

"Yeah!" shot back Santo, staring straight ahead at Allen in the batter's box.

Selma went into the stretch. As the runners started moving, he took his foot off the rubber. Selma whirled and lobbed the ball toward third. There was no balk call.

The ball sailed into foul territory. Santo was nowhere near the bag. One runner scored, the other took third, and the Phils went on to win.

Afterwards, a furious Leo Durocher ordered coach Joey Amalfitano to find out why Selma had thrown to third. Selma explained the trick play, including the sign and countersign. Next, Amalfitano confronted Santo, who said they'd talked about the play earlier in the year.

"Know what the sign is?" Amalfitano asked.

Santo pondered the question for a few seconds, then replied: "Yeah. He tells me to knock the ball down."

"Did you answer him," asked the coach.

"Holy cow!" exclaimed Santo, finally realizing he'd completely spaced it. "I answered him!"

Hank Sauer

B efore Henry Aaron claimed it, the nickname "Hammerin' Hank," belonged to Hank Sauer, the Cubs' slugging out-fielder from 1949 to 1955.

The rawboned 6'2", 200-pound Pittsburgh native was the second member of his family to play in Cubs livery.

S auer broke into organized baseball in 1937 as a first baseman in the New York Yankees chain. He reached the majors with Cincinnati in 1941, playing nine games in the outfield. He got into seven more in 1942 as a first basemen.

After spending all of 1943 with Syracuse of the International League, Sauer joined the Coast Guard. He was out of baseball until Word War II ended in August 1945. He rejoined the Reds, playing in 31 games.

Dispatched to the minors prior to the '46 season, Sauer spent the next two years in Syracuse. He was the I.L.'s most valuable player in 1947, batting .336 with 50 home runs and 141 runs batted in.

The following year Sauer took over as the Reds' left fielder. He evolved into one of the majors' top sluggers, producing 35 homers and 97 RBIs.

In June 1949 the Reds dealt Sauer to Chicago in a four-player swap. Soon, Hammerin' Hank would pick up another nickname: Mayor of Wrigley Field.

A favorite of Chicago fans, Sauer averaged better than 30 homers a season in his first six years as a Cub, including a career-high 41 in '54.

When the pipe-smoking Sauer would return to his fielder's post after each round-tripper, Wrigley Field bleacher fans would strew the outfield with packets of tobacco.

Sauer's prominent proboscis made him a favorite target of bench jockeys around the league.

Leo Durocher, who claimed Sauer's nose resembled an automobile hood ornament, was one of Hank's worst tormentors. Every time Sauer stepped up to the plate against one of Durocher's teams, Leo would yell, "Hey, Pontiac!"

Sauer would have to call time and step out of the box to regain his composure.

During the 1950s, Sauer was involved in two acrimonious controversies.

He was elected by fans to the 1950 N.L. All-Star team along with outfielders Enos Slaughter of the Cardinals and Pittsburgh's Ralph Kiner. But Brooklyn's Burt Shotton, manager of the N.L. squad, wasn't happy about having three left fielders in the starting line-up.

Shotton announced plans to start his own center fielder, Duke Snider, with Sauer going to the bench.

Shotton's decision set off howls of protest in Chicago, where the All-Star contest was to take place at Comiskey Park. *Chicago Tribune* sports editor Arch Ward, the man who helped launch the annual midsummer classic back in 1933, blasted Shotton. The Dodger skipper, claimed Ward, was "telling 781,553 fans who supported Sauer they are wrong and he is right." Shotton eventually relented and Sauer was the starting right fielder in the N.L.'s 14-inning 4-3 triumph.

At the All-Star game at Philadelphia two years later, Hank's homer off Cleveland's Bob Lemon gave the N.L. a 3-2 win in a five-inning, rain-shortened contest.

After the season, the announcement of Sauer as the N.L. MVP for 1952 touched off a firestorm that made the '50 All-Star game controversy seem like a picnic.

Sauer had tied for the N.L. homer lead with 37, and his 121 ribbies led both leagues. The MVP ballot showed 226 points for Sauer, who received eight of a possible 24 first-place votes.

Phillies pitcher Robin Roberts, a 28-game winner, earned seven first-place votes and a 211-point total. Several Eastern writers claimed Roberts deserved the award, and demanded a recount.

I n the *Chicago Sun-Times,* columnist Edgar Munzel defended the Mayor of Wrigley Field's MVP credentials.

"What anguished screams are emanating from the east," wrote Munzel, "because of the selection of Hank Sauer over Robin Roberts . . . It's pure sour grapes that should be crushed underfoot. In my estimation, the choice of Sauer was one of the soundest ever made . . ."

T he Cubs sent Sauer to St. Louis after the 1955 season in an unpopular trade.

He played for the Giants in 1957, their last year in New York, and moved west to San Francisco with the team for 1958, his final season.

E d Sauer, Hank's younger brother, was also a major leaguer. Ed played for the Cubs from 1943 to 1945 and spent time with the Cardinals and Braves in 1949.

Sammy Sosa

Cubs right fielder Sammy Sosa demolished more than just N.L. pitching during 1998.

He also destroyed a baseball shibboleth that stereotypes Dominican players good-field, no-hit middle infielders.

Over the years, the Dominican Republic has produced hard-hitting outfielders like George Bell and the Alou brothers, Felipe, Jesus and Mateo, and multi-position thumpers like Rico Carty and Pedro Guerrero . . . not to mention hard-throwing hurlers like Juan Marichal and Joaquin Andujar.

Ossie Virgil, the first Dominican-born big leaguer, wasn't a second baseman or a shortstop, but a catcher.

But then came Manny Alexander. Mariano Duncan. Tony Fernandez. Julio Franco. Pedro Gonzalez. Alfredo Griffin. Julian Javier. Manny Lee. Nelson Norman. Rafael Ramirez. Rafael Robles. Amado Samuel. All middle infielders, and all from the

sugar-producing municipality of San Pedro de Macoris in southeastern Santo Domingo.

Right-handed hitting Sammy Sosa also hails from San Pedro de Macoris. He was discovered by Omar Minaya, then a scout for the Rangers and today one of baseball's top executives.

In those days, Samuel Peralta Sosa was known as "Mikey," a nickname bestowed by his grandmother. When he wasn't shining shoes or selling oranges, little Mikey played baseball—usually with a broken broomstick for a bat and a ball made of soap wrapped in a sock.

Sosa signed with Texas in 1986 and, three years later when he joined the Rangers at age 19, his 6'0", 150-pound frame appeared better suited for shortstop than right field. Scouts raved about his great speed and range, his arm and his power.

In July 1989 Texas dealt Sosa to the White Sox in a five-player trade. The Cubs acquired Sammy and pitcher Ken Patterson in a trade for George Bell on the last day of March in 1992.

Sosa split the '92 season between the Cubs and Iowa of the American Association. He hit 33 home runs in 1993, his first full season with the Cubs.

He followed with homer totals of 25 in strike-curtailed 1994; 36 in 1995; 40 in 1996; and 36 in 1997.

B y 1998 Sosa had filled out to a muscular 210 pounds. That summer, he and St. Louis first baseman Mark McGwire hooked up in one of the greatest home run duels of all time.

Sosa and McGwire became only the third and fourth sluggers to surpass the 60-homer mark. McGwire finished with 70, while Sosa hit 66. Both men bettered the 37-year-old major league mark of 61 by Roger Maris of the Yankees.

Sosa and McGwire staged another homer-fest in 1999. The pair again topped the 60-mark, with McGwire coming out on top, 65 to 63.

B ut for chance, Sosa may have been playing in Philadelphia or Toronto. When Sosa was 15, he signed a contract with the Phillies. The contract was illegal, however, since professional baseball rules prohibit players under 16 from turning pro.

When the mistake was discovered, the contract was voided. Soon afterwards Sosa began working out at a Blue Jays camp in the Dominican Republic. Spotting Sosa arriving daily at the rival Blue Jays' field, the quick-witted Omar Minaya developed a plan.

"I had someone wait for him at the bus stop by the Jays' camp," confesses Minaya, "and when he got off the bus we shipped him three hours across the island and signed him to a contract with the Rangers."

Four years after snatching Sosa away from the Jays, Minaya projected Sosa as a power hitter. "He's going to hit 30 home runs," Minaya told a newspaper reporter.

Thirty home runs?

Even if he was a tad weak on his projections, Minaya sure knew talent when he saw it.

Al Spalding

A nyone who set foot on a schoolyard playground during the middle years of the Twentieth Century remembers playing with hollow, bright pink rubber balls. Known as "Spaldeens," those balls were as common to generations of young Americans as bubblegum, baseball cards, and braces.

"Spaldeen" was a corruption of the name of the firm that made the balls—the A.G. Spalding sporting goods company, which also produced the official baseball of the National League.

S ports historians will also recognize the name Spalding from the series of baseball guide books. The Spalding baseball guide series provided an annual recapitulation of the previous year's season, complete with statistics and commentary.

The man behind this conglomerate was Illinois native Albert G. Spalding (1850-1915), a skilled businessman and promoter who organized the world's first baseball tour in 1888-1889.

Spalding was also manager, club secretary, president and, eventually, owner of Chicago's N.L. franchise. The multi-talented Spalding was even a member of the 1900 U.S. Olympic shooting team.

In his younger days, Al Spalding was an outstanding baseball pitcher. He earned the win in Chicago's first game, a 4-0 win over Louisville on April 25, 1876.

The right-hander was also the winning pitcher in Chicago's first home game on May 10, 1876, a 6-0 triumph over Cincinnati at 23rd and State Streets.

Al Spalding, a skillful politician and diplomat, and an excellent organizer as well, was elected to baseball's Hall of Fame in 1939.

He was also responsible for one of baseball's earliest fiascos. In 1882 Spalding came up with an idea for color-coded uniforms—not by team, but by position!

According to Spalding's scheme, the color of each player's cap and shirt would identify where he played on the diamond. The color code was as follows: baby blue, pitchers; scarlet, catchers; scarlet and white, first basemen; orange and black, second basemen; blue and white, third basemen; maroon, shortstops; gray, right fielders; red and black, center fielders; white, left fielders.

All players wore white belts, pants, and ties.

So how were fans supposed to figure out a player's team? By the color of his socks.

Fortunately, Spalding's experiment didn't last beyond the 1882 season.

Eddie Stanky

One of the toughest, smartest players of his time, Eddie Stanky reached the majors with the Cubs in 1943. Nicknamed "The Brat", Stanky also played for the Dodgers, Giants, Braves, and Cardinals in an 11-year career, and also managed St. Louis, the White Sox, and the Texas Rangers.

Leo Durocher appreciated Stanky's drive and determination. When Stanky played second base for Leo in Brooklyn, Durocher lauded the 5'8", 170-pound pepperpot.

"Look at 'The Brat'," said Durocher. "He can't hit, can't run, can't field. He's no nice guy, but all the little guy can do is win."

Durocher compared Stanky to Mel Ott, the slugging outfielder who was managing the Giants at the time. Leo pointed out that Ott, on the other hand, was a nice guy, but finished second.

Somehow, these words morphed into "Nice guys finish last"—something Durocher never actually said. Yet when Leo penned his autobiography, he entitled it *Nice Guys Finish Last.*

Peanuts Lowery was on hand during the feisty rookie's early days with the Cubs. He remembered Rip Sewell of Pittsburgh beaning Stanky, who went down in a heap.

"We all ran out, of course," Lowery recalled. "Stanky looked awful woozy and the doctor, after some first aid, started asking him what day it was, how many fingers was he holding up and so forth."

The plucky Stanky bounced up and shook off the ministrations of the doctor and his teammates.

"Nuts to that stuff, Doc!" spat Stanky. "I'm all right."

Stanky refused to come out of the game, got up and trotted off to first base. On the very next pitch, he took off for second and slid into the bag.

"He hit shortstop Huck Geary so hard," claimed Lowery, "he broke the guy's leg!"

Harry Steinfeldt

These are the saddest of possible words:
"Tinker-to-Evers-to-Chance."
Trio of bear cubs, and fleeter than birds,
"Tinker-to-Evers-to-Chance."
Ruthlessly pricking our gonfalon bubble,
Making a Giant hit into a double—
Words that are weighty with nothing but trouble:
"Tinker-to-Evers-to-Chance."

*B*aseball's Sad Lexicon, Franklin P. Adams' ode to the Cubs'
    great infield ran in the *New York Evening Mail* in July 1910
and became a baseball classic.

Although not mentioned in Adams' poem, Harry
Steinfeldt played third base alongside Joe Tinker, Johnny Evers,
and Frank Chance from 1906 to 1910.

A St. Louis native who originally hoped to make his mark in
theater, Steinfeldt played in four World Series with the Cubs

and batted .471 (8-for-17) in Chicago's four-game sweep of Detroit in 1907.

S teinfeldt broke in with Cincinnati in 1898 and was a steady, if unspectacular, mainstay in the Reds' infield through 1905. His 32 doubles led the N.L. in 1903, a year he batted .312.

Injuries limited Steinfeldt to 99 games in 1904 and the Reds, figuring Harry's best days were behind him, dealt him to Chicago for third baseman Hans Lobert and pitcher Jake Weimer in March 1906.

T he change of scenery rejuvenated the 28-year-old infielder. Steinfeldt hit a career-best .327 in his first year in Chicago and helped the Cubs win 116 games.

His 176 hits and 83 runs batted in topped the N.L. During Harry's five years of service in Chicago, the Cubs won four pennants and two World Series.

"Steiny" once played an entire 15-inning game without handling a single chance at third base.

H arry's presence helped solidify the Cubs as the favorite team of one segment of Chicago's population.

With players like Steinfeldt, Solly Hofman, Johnny Kling, Jack Pfiester, Ed Reulbach, Frank "Wildfire" Schulte, Jimmy Sheckard, and Heinie Zimmerman on the roster, the Cubs were the darlings of the city's German-American community.

Steinfeldt was traded to the Boston Braves after the 1910 season and played just 19 games in 1911 before bowing out of the majors.

He was the first member of the glamorous infield to pass on. A few years after retirement, he became ill, and in time had to be confined to a sanitarium. Released in August 1914, Steinfeldt returned to his home in Bellevue, Kentucky, just across from Cincinnati. He died there soon after, at age 36.

Harry Steinfeldt deserved better treatment than omission from *Baseball's Sad Lexicon.*

Grantland Rice, after all, paid homage to the entire Notre Dame backfield of Crowley, Layden, Miller, and Stuhldreher, and the thought of the Apocalyptic Horsemen without mention of Pestilence or Famine is unthinkable.

The following lines are dedicated to the memory of the Cubs' stalwart, albeit snubbed, infielder:

> *Here's evidence justice will sometime miscarry,*
> *"Tinker-to-Evers-to-Chance."*
> *The Cubs' infield ode fails to mention poor Harry,*
> *"Tinker-to-Evers-to-Chance."*

Chicago's third baseman, just as sublime,
As Chance, Evers or Tinker . . . most of the time.
Left out because Steinfeldt's unwieldy in rhyme,
"Tinker-to-Evers-to-Chance."

Riggs Stephenson

S ome say superb fielders are ignored when it's time for Hall of
Fame balloting. Cooperstown, they maintain, favors offensive
players.

Maybe so. But how, then, do you account for Riggs
Stephenson?

S tephenson, a star fullback for the University of Alabama,
reached the major leagues with Cleveland in 1921 as a second
baseman. An arm injury from his football days hampered
Stephenson's throwing, but not his bat.

He averaged .371 in 74 games for the Indians in 1924.

Stephenson went to the minors to become an outfielder. When Riggs played for Kansas City and Indianapolis in the American Association, Joe McCarthy managed Louisville. And when McCarthy became Chicago's manager in 1926, he demanded that the Cubs acquire Stephenson's contract.

From 1929 to 1931, the Cubs boasted one of baseball's finest outfields with Kiki Cuyler in right, Hack Wilson in center, and Stephenson in left. Stephenson never hit below .319 for the Cubs except for 1934, his final big league season, when he batted just 74 times in 38 games. Starting in '26, Stephenson hit .338, .344, .324, .362, .367, .319, .324, and .329. In two World Series, he batted .378—.319 against the Athletics in '29, and .444 against the Yankees in '32.

Never a power hitter, Stephenson's top homer mark was 17 in '29. He led the N.L. with 46 doubles in '27.

Umpire Ernie Quigley was Stephenson's fraternity brother. Whenever Quigley called a strike on Stephenson, Riggs would gently chide him, saying "That was a little outside, wasn't it, Ernie?"

One day, after Stephenson commented after a close pitch, Quigley replied: "My boy, I'd rather call them on you than on anyone else."

"Yes," shot back Riggs, "but if you keep calling them like that on me, I won't be around here very long!"

Teammate Woody English said he couldn't understand how Kiki Cuyler could be elected to the Hall of Fame, while Stephenson had been passed over.

English said that if Stephenson came to the plate in the bottom of the ninth with the bases loaded and the lead run aboard, "we'd put our gloves in our pockets and go up the runway to the clubhouse. He would drive that winning run in time after time."

Stephenson's .336 career batting average with Chicago is the highest of any Cub player. The lifelong Alabaman had good memories of Cub fans.

"They were very nice to me," he recalled. "I couldn't have played in a better place."

Rick Sutcliffe

Twice in Chicago history, American League castoffs have pitched the Cubs into post-season play.

In late July 1945, right-hander Hank Borowy came over from the Yankees. Borowy's 11-2 record down the stretch helped the Cubs win the N.L. pennant. A 10-5 record in New York gave the Fordham University product 21 wins on the season.

Thirty-nine years later at Wrigley Field, lightning struck again. Midway through 1984, the Cleveland Indians were ready to unload Rick Sutcliffe, a 6'7", 215-pound right-hander.

Sutcliffe had won 17 games for Los Angeles in 1979, and four years later had matched that figure with the Indians. The Tribe traded Sutcliffe, reliever George Frazier and catcher Ron Hassey to the Cubs for outfielders Joe Carter and Mel Hall, along with pitchers Don Schulze and Darryl Banks.

The change of scenery worked like a tonic on Sutcliffe.
Struggling at 4-5 with Cleveland, the former N.L. Rookie of the Year went 16-1 for the Cubs. During one stretch he won 14 consecutive decisions.

The Cubs charged to the N.L. East title, appearing in post-season play for the first time since '45. Sutcliffe, with a combined record of 20-6 with the Indians and Cubs, became the first pitcher since Borowy to win 20 games after changing leagues in mid-season.

Rick's heroics earned him the '84 N.L. Cy Young Award. In 1989 his 16-11 slate helped the Cubs win another division title.

Sut remained in Chicago through 1991 and retired after the 1994 season after doing time with Baltimore and St. Louis.

One of the big redhead's most unforgettable moments as a Cub happened against the Phillies on July 29, 1988.

On a steamy night at Veterans Stadium, the Cubs took a 3-2 lead into the top of the seventh. Sutcliffe, a good hitter, opened the inning with a double to left center. After Shawon Dunston flied out, Sutcliffe rumbled into third on Manny Trillo's deep drive to right.

Phillies pitcher Kevin Gross walked the following batter, Mitch Webster. On his next delivery, Gross threw to first and caught Webster off base. Seeing an opportunity, Sutcliffe—who would never make anyone forget Lou Brock—took off for home.

Phils first baseman Ricky Jordan, stunned by the sight of the mammoth Sutcliffe churning toward the plate, threw the ball into the Cubs dugout. Sutcliffe scored, and the umpires waved Webster around.

Webster was credited with a steal of second and Jordan was charged with a throwing error. Sutcliffe, too, got a stolen base on the play.

"You guys shouldn't be surprised," said a straight-faced Sutcliffe afterwards. "I stole a base last year, too."

Sutcliffe became the first Cubs pitcher in 69 years to steal home.

The last to do it? Another terror of the basepaths, Jim "Hippo" Vaughn.

Bruce Sutter

B ruce Sutter was an outstanding athlete at Donegal High
School in Mount Joy, Pennsylvania. He was the football
team's quarterback, he captained the basketball squad and pitched
for the baseball team.

In 1972 Sutter signed with the Cubs. Soon afterward, he
suffered an elbow injury that required off-season surgery.

S utter reported to Quincy of the Midwest League in 1973. His
arm was still tender, however, and Sutter was reluctant to
throw any kind of breaking pitch. He was relying strictly on
fastballs, and the Chicago brass figured he was, at best, a marginal
prospect.

That changed after Fred Martin visited Quincy. Martin,
the former Cubs pitching coach, was by then a roving minor
league pitching instructor. Martin talked Sutter into trying the

split-fingered fastball. That pitch would turn Sutter into one of the game's most effective relief pitchers.

S utter joined the Cubs after compiling a 1.75 ERA over his next two-and-a-half seasons. His split-finger, which dropped suddenly when it reached home plate, was nearly unhittable.

Sutter rapidly developed into one of baseball's most effective closers. He was the winning pitcher in the 1978 and 1979 All-Star Games. Sutter won the N.L. Cy Young Award in '79.

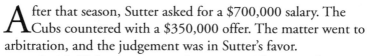

A fter that season, Sutter asked for a $700,000 salary. The Cubs countered with a $350,000 offer. The matter went to arbitration, and the judgement was in Sutter's favor.

Baseball's landscape was changing rapidly. Just a few years earlier, Sutter's salary had been in the $20,000 range. Bill Wrigley, a scion of the family that had owned the Cubs for decades, saw the writing on the wall.

In June 1981, Wrigley sold the team to the Chicago Tribune Company for $20.5 million.

S utter helped the Cardinals win the 1982 World Series, and finished his career in 1988 after a stint with the Braves. Yet Wrigley Field would always have a special place in his heart.

"Cubs fans are exceptional, whether you're in first place or last place," maintains Sutter. "They are the most loyal fans in the United States. I enjoyed Chicago a lot."

Tony Taylor

Tony Taylor, a 19-year big league second baseman, began his career with Chicago in 1958.

He was the Cubs second baseman from '58 through May 1960, when he was swapped to Philadelphia along with catcher Cal Neeman for pitcher Don Cardwell and first baseman Ed Bouchee.

In 2,195 big league contests, the Cuban native hit just 75 home runs, 15 of them in a Chicago uniform.

The Cubs' bullpen deserves credit for one of them.

At Wrigley Field on July 1, 1958, Taylor and Ernie Banks both had a pair of home runs against the Giants. One of

Taylor's homers was a smash just inside third base that bounced into the Cub bullpen and then into a rain gutter at the base of the left field grandstand wall.

Taylor's drive scattered the Cubs' bullpen corps. As San Francisco left fielder Leon Wagner rushed toward the scene, the Chicago players peered intently under the bullpen bench as if the ball were still there. Wagner scrambled around the bench looking for the ball, when it was actually 40' or 50' farther down the line in the gutter.

By the time Wagner found the ball, Taylor was around the bases. The Cubs won the game, 9-5.

Tinker to Evers to Chance

Together, shortstop Joe Tinker, second baseman Johnny Evers and first baseman Frank Chance started for the Cubs for eight full seasons. They collaborated on their first double play on September 15, 1902.

During their tenure the Cubs won pennants in 1906, 1907, 1908, and 1910, and World Series titles in '07 and '08. All three took turns as manager of the Cubs, and the trio was elected to baseball's Hall of Fame in the same year.

Franklin P. Adams' famous poem earned them another slice of immortality. It's easy to think of Tinker, Evers, and Chance as a single entity, a homogenous, open-the-box-and-snap-together unit.

Nothing could be further from the truth.

Frank Chance played for Chicago from 1898 to 1912. Chance was a dental student at the University of Washington when he was discovered by Bill Lange, Chicago's star outfielder of the 1890s.

A catcher, Chance languished on the bench until 1902. Since Chance suffered frequent injuries behind the plate, manager Frank Selee suggested a move to first base. Chance wouldn't hear of it, and threatened to quit when Selee ordered him to make the switch. Chance relented, however, and developed into one of the deadball era's top first basemen. His best year was 1903, when he batted .327 and stole 67 bases.

Tough, smart and a fierce competitor, Chance succeeded Selee as manager in 1905. Dubbed "the Peerless Leader," he was a demanding field boss who led the Cubs to four pennants and a pair of World Series victories. His 1906 team won an amazing 116 regular-season games, a mark that still stands. Chance was also a hard-knuckled disciplinarian who pummeled opposing players (and his own men as well) if he thought they had it coming.

Chance left Chicago on a sour note. When owner Charles Murphy criticized Chance's players for carousing during the 1912 season, Chance lambasted Murphy as a cheapskate. Soon after, Chance was gone from the Cubs. He later managed the Yankees and Red Sox.

Johnny Evers (pronounced like "weavers") was known as "The Crab" for the way he scuttled around second base . . . as well as an abrasive disposition that rivaled Ty Cobb's. Like Cobb, Evers had no qualms about spiking opponents who got in his way.

A native of Troy, New York, Evers came to Chicago in 1902. He was a quick thinker and a sure-handed second baseman, but a light hitter. Still, Evers could rise to the occasion. In both the 1907 and 1908 World Series he batted .350.

In 1913 he took over from Chance as Cubs manager. Like Chance, however, Evers quarreled with Charles Murphy and was soon gone. In 1914 he managed Boston's "Miracle Braves" to an N.L. pennant and a World Series title. He returned briefly to Chicago in 1921 for another stint as Cubs manager.

Like most of the Cubs players, Evers had a great respect and admiration for Frank Chance.

His relationship with shortstop Joe Tinker was another matter.

Like Evers, *Joe Tinker* came to Chicago in 1902. And, like Evers, he was considered an artist in the field, but a weak hitter—yet one who came through in the clutch, just like his keystone partner.

In 1908 Tinker hit the first home run by a Cub in World Series play. Against the great Christy Mathewson of the Giants, he had a lifetime .291 average. In his time, Tinker was ranked second at shortstop only to Pittsburgh's Honus Wagner.

Tinker was an aggressive competitor, as were Chance and Evers. He may not have been as quick with his fists, but Tinker could hold his own in any rumble.

After a game with Cincinnati, Dick Egan of the Reds challenged him. Tinker, who had already dressed, removed his coat and squared off. The fight lasted five minutes, and Tinker completely thrashed Egan.

After the fight, said witnesses, Tinker's hair wasn't even mussed.

The Cubs sent Tinker to the Reds in an eight-player deal in December 1912. Tinker jumped to Chicago of the Federal League for the 1914 and 1915 seasons, then returned to the Cubs as player-manager in 1916.

Like Chance and Evers, Tinker's first hitch with the Cubs ended acrimoniously. He asked to be traded when Evers was named manager.

The two had rarely spoken to each other since September 1905, when they got into a fight during an exhibition game in Bedford, Indiana. The problem centered around a ride from their hotel to the ballpark. Tinker had left by himself in a hack, leaving Evers and others standing at the curb. Evers wasn't happy about it. When he finally made it the park, Evers told off Tinker.

Tempers simmered until the middle of the game, when the pair locked horns right on the diamond. Teammates broke up the fight, but Evers was still fuming over the curbside snub. A day after the fight, Evers told Tinker they'd be better off just doing their jobs, but not speaking to one another unless it was absolutely necessary.

"That suits me," is what Tinker is said to have replied.

"It was unfortunate," Evers said years later. "I figured that if he wanted that way, he could have it."

And that's the way it continued, season after season, through four pennants and two championship seasons. Tinker and Evers played side by side for the next five seasons, avoiding each other as much as possible.

After their playing days, the hard feelings softened. At Cooperstown in 1946, Evers and Tinker stood together one more time as they were inducted into the Hall of Fame.

"Joe was there when I walked in," said Evers. "We hadn't seen each other for years. And do you know what we did? We rushed together, threw our arms around each other and cried like a couple of kids."

Chance, who died in 1924 at age 47, was inducted posthumously.

"I'm glad we made it all together," said Evers. "Chance should have been elected long ago. I wish he were alive to feel as happy about it as I do. I'm glad for Tinker, too."

When a Chicago newspaper reporter researched the number of twin killings by the celebrated trio, he came up with some astonishing numbers. Between 1906 and 1909, they combined for just 54 double plays—29 initiated by Tinker, the rest by Evers. Comparison with modern double play figures, however, doesn't work.

In an era when stolen bases and sacrifice bunts were the order of the day—and when pitchers put more trust in fly-ball outs, rather than grounders on rough infields—double plays were much more scarce.

Evers died less than a year later, and Tinker passed on in 1948. Together with Chance, they live on as the most celebrated infield in baseball history.

Chuck Tolson

After breaking in with the Indians in 1925, first baseman Chuck Tolson moved on to Chicago the following year and played for the Cubs in 1926-1927 and 1929-30. In 1927 Tolson was the N.L.'s top pinch hitter with 14 hits in 40 at-bats.

One year later, he made Cubs history while batting in a pinch.

In the seventh inning of a game with Pittsburgh at Forbes Field on May 1, 1927, Chicago manager Joe McCarthy sent Tolson up to hit against right-hander Ray Kremer with the bases loaded.

Tolson responded with a home run, becoming the first Cub ever to pinch-hit a grand slam. Tolson had just four homers in his 144 big league contests, but was 23-for-74 lifetime as a pinch batter.

Tolson's grand slam heroics, however, went for naught. The Cubs lost, 7-6, in the bottom of the ninth when Charlie Root walked the bases full and Pittsburgh's Paul Waner singled home the tying and winning runs.

Hippo Vaughn

Jim "Hippo" Vaughn, a 6'4," 215-pound Texan, pitched 13 years in majors, including a hitch with the Cubs from 1913 to 1921. He won 20 games or more five times for Chicago.

In 1918 he led the N.L. with 22 victories and a 1.74 ERA, and helped the Cubs to a pennant.

Vaughn, whose nickname stemmed from his lumbering gait, is best remembered for a May 2, 1917, contest at Weeghman Park (as Wrigley Field was known until 1926), when he hooked up with Fred Toney in one of the greatest pitching duels in history.

"I'd always given Toney's team, Cincinnati, a fit, so this day they laid for me," Vaughn said years later. The Reds loaded their lineup with right-handed batters against the southpaw Vaughn, even benching left-handed hitting Edd Roush, a future Hall of Famer.

For nine innings, Vaughn and Toney threw hitless ball. The game was scoreless with the Reds coming to bat in the top of the 10th.

"I knew I was tired," said Vaughn, "but I felt that I still had my stuff."

Vaughn retired the leadoff man but the next batter, Larry Kopf, got the game's first hit. One out later, Hal Chase hit a fly ball that Chicago center fielder Cy Williams dropped. After Kopf went to third on the error, Chase stole second. Cincinnati's Jim Thorpe, the great track and field star of the 1912 Olympics, sent a swinging bunt toward third.

"I knew the minute it was hit that I couldn't get Thorpe at first," said Vaughn. "He was as fast as a race horse."

Vaughn tried to nail Kopf at the plate, but the throw hit catcher Art Wilson's chest protector and dropped to the ground. Chase tried to score on the play, but Wilson tagged him out. Toney set down the Cubs in order in the bottom of the 10th to preserve his no-hitter.

"I don't believe he ever beat me again," Vaughn said of Toney years later. "We met a lot of times, and most of the games were close, but he had licked me for the last time."

Vaughn is best remembered for the near double no-hitter. All but forgotten, however, are Vaughn's pitching heroics in the World Series. He won one game and lost two against the Red Sox in 1918, with an earned run average of 1.00.

The World Series of 1918 took place in early September. The United States had entered World War I, and the government had issued a "work-or-fight" order that threatened to put every able-bodied major leaguer either at work in a defense plant or in uniform.

The government gave the major leagues until the end of August to finish the season, and another couple of weeks' grace to play the Series.

The Cubs, who finished the season 84-45, opened the Series at home against the Red Sox. Vaughn gave up just one run in the fourth inning on a walk and two singles. It was the lone score in a 1-0 Red Sox triumph.

After the Cubs evened the Series, Vaughn started Game Three at home on September 7. Boston won another squeaker, this time by a 2-1 margin behind Carl Mays.

Three days later in Boston, the Cubs had their backs to the wall. The Red Sox had won the fourth game, and one more Boston victory would have ended the Series. Once again, Cubs manager Fred Mitchell went with Vaughn. Vaughn responded with another stellar performance. This time, the big right-hander threw a 5-hit shutout to beat Boston's Sam Jones, 3-0.

It was all for naught, however. The following day, the Red Sox won 2-1 to take the Series. And the Boston pitcher who beat Vaughn in the 1-0 game? He was a 23-year-old southpaw named Babe Ruth.

Jerome Walton and Dwight Smith

The longest Cubs hitting streak between 1900 and 1999 is 30 games, by:

A. Rogers Hornsby
B. Stan Hack
C. Billy Williams
D. Ryne Sandberg
E. None of the above

The answer is E. The longest Cubs hit streak during the 20th Century belongs to Jerome Walton, a right-handed hitting outfielder for the Cubs from 1989 through 1992.

Bill Dahlen, a 19th Century star, had hitting streaks of 28 and 42 in 1894.

Prior to Walton, the top hit skein by a Cub in the 1900s was 28 by Ron Santo in 1966.

Outfielders Jerome Walton and Dwight Smith hooked up in Chicago in 1989. They batted in the top two spots in the Cub line-up, earning the nickname "The Daily Double".

During spring camp that year in Arizona, Smith couldn't find himself. He batted .259, made three errors and was farmed out.

"You'll never see that Dwight Smith again," he vowed.

Walton made the jump from Double-A Pittsfield in '89 as a 23-year-old. He began the season in center field, but a hamstring injury cost him 30 games during May and June.

The 25-year-old Smith, in the meantime, tore up the American Association at a .325 clip and was recalled after 21 games.

When Walton came off the disabled list in June, the two took over the top two spots in the batting order. Walton manned center, with Smith in left.

While Smith was outgoing and a clubhouse comic, Walton was more reserved. He soared like a meteor in '89, but flamed out just as quickly.

Walton batted .293 in his first season, and won N.L. Rookie of the Year honors. Smith hit .324 in 109 games.

A fter winning the Eastern Division title in '89, the 1990 season was a bust for the Cubs as they dropped into a tie for fourth place. At one point the entire Chicago outfield—Walton, Smith, and right fielder Andre Dawson—was on the DL.

Walton and Smith were disappointments. Walton tailed off to .263 in '90, however, and his average plummeted to .219 in 1991. After hitting .127 in 30 games for Chicago in '92, Walton was gone from Wrigley Field.

S mith slumped to .262 in '90. Although he batted .276 in '92 and an even .300 in '91, he never lived up to the promise he showed as a rookie. After a .262 average in 1993, he was dispatched to the California Angels.

Billy Williams

B illy Williams is the man who forced Ernie Banks out of left
field in Wrigley Field.

Ernie Banks? *Left field???*

In 1961, when his legs began to wear out, Chicago's
College of Coaches tinkered with the idea of making a left fielder
out of Ernie.

T he '61 season was Billy Williams' rookie year. He'd been
with the Cubs for a couple of cups of coffee in 1959 and
1960.

A .323 average and 26 homers for Houston of the American Association, coupled with a brilliant Spring Training performance in '61, brought the sweet-swinging Alabaman to Chicago
for good.

S hunted between right and left field, Williams muddled through the early going. Vedie Himsl, the head coach at the time, shifted Banks from short to left on May 23. From then through the middle of June, Williams spent most of his time riding the bench.

He did go 5-for-8 as a pinch hitter, however, and in mid-June general manager John Holland sent word to the dugout: get Williams in the lineup every day, for at least a month.

O n June 16, the Cubs opened a three-game series at San Francisco. Banks—who hated playing the outfield—was shifted to first. Andre Rodgers played short, George Altman was in right and Williams took over in left.

Billy responded with a grand slam homer in the Cubs' 12-6 win. He had 10 hits in his next 19 at-bats, and was in the lineup for good. He batted .278 with 25 homers and 86 RBI, earning the N.L. Rookie of the Year Award.

W illiams hit 20 or more homers for 13 consecutive seasons. He had 30 or more five times during that stretch, including a career-high 42 in 1970.

In a line-up that included Banks, Ron Santo, Glenn Beckert, Don Kessinger, and Randy Hundley, Williams sparked the Cubs' renaissance in the late '60s and early '70s. A perennial All-Star, he was named Major League Player of the Year by *The Sporting News* in 1972.

During his early years with the Cubs, Williams would toss his glove into the stands after the last game of the season. "To make some kid happy," he explained. Williams would then break in a new glove during Spring Training.

After Fergie Jenkins joined the Cubs, Williams would turn over his old gloves to him. Jenkins collected equipment for distribution to needy youngsters.

"A few years ago," Billy relates, "I got one of my gloves back. I now keep it in a Plexiglas box."

Williams conducted an unusual ritual when he came in from the field knowing he'd be coming up to bat. He would chew half a stick of gum and, as he'd walk around the catcher on his way to the plate, he would spit out the wad and swing at it.

Williams' theory was that if he could hit a little piece of gum, he should be able to hit a baseball.

One of Williams' greatest feats was a playing streak of 1,117 games. The streak began September 22, 1963, and lasted until September 3, 1970. It set an N.L. record (since topped by Steve Garvey) for consecutive games played.

After the 1974 season the Cubs dealt Williams to Oakland, where he played two more seasons, mostly as a designated hitter. In 1987 Williams was inducted into the Hall of Fame. He eventually returned to the Cubs as a batting instructor.

Sportswriter Bill Gleason paid homage to Williams in his *Chicago Sun-Times* column. "He combines the dignity of Ernie Banks," wrote Gleason, "the determination of Santo, and the competitive fires of Hundley, and he plays every day, every night."

Ned Williamson

B abe Ruth of the Boston Red Sox hit 29 homers in 1919, a new major league mark. The record he broke was 27, by Chicago infielder Ned Williamson in 1884.

But talk about cheap home runs! In 1884 Chicago's home field was Lakefront Park. There, the right field fence was 230 feet from home plate. Until 1883, any ball hit over the wall in right was a ground rule double. The rule changed in 1884, and any ball over the right field fence was a homer.

I n the second game of a double header on May 30, Williamson hit three home runs in Chicago's 12-2 victory over Detroit. Williamson's triple-homer performance was the first-ever by a big league player.

Of his 27 homers in 1884, all but two came at Lakefront Park. The following year, when the Chicago squad moved to West Side Park, Williamson's homer total dropped to three.

Primarily a third baseman-shortstop, Williamson spent 13 years in the majors. From 1878 through 1883 he hit eight homers. From 1885 to 1890 he had 28. Of his 67 career home runs, 43 percent came during that 1884 season at Lakefront Park.

In his time, Williamson was as popular with the fans as Ernie Banks would be decades later.

Cap Anson called him "the greatest all-around ballplayer the country ever saw," and said Williamson was "a big, good-natured and good-hearted fellow."

Williamson was an excellent fielder. He was also—to Anson's chagrin—a *bon vivant* who took full advantage of Chicago's social opportunities.

He was also a superstitious man. Whenever he needed a turn of luck, Williamson would find a pebble and place it under the foul side of third base.

Williamson suffered a knee injury in France during Al Spalding's world tour in 1888-1889. He never fully recovered, and was gone from the big leagues after the 1890 campaign.

Williamson died in 1894 at age 38. "He could do more with a baseball," wrote sportswriter C.G. Perkins, "than anybody I ever saw, and I have seen them all."

Hack Wilson

H ack Wilson drove home 1,063 runs during his 12-year big league career. He picked up his last one in 1999.
Pretty impressive for a guy who died in 1948.

W ilson was one of the most exciting players in Chicago history. Built like a fireplug at 5'6" and 190 pounds, Wilson had powerful arms and shoulders that enabled him to hit 56 home runs in 1930—an N.L. record that stood until 1998.

W ilson played for the Cubs from 1926 through 1931. He averaged .307 in Chicago, including a career-high .356 in 1930, and helped the Cubs to the 1929 N.L. flag. Despite his odd build—a barrel-thick body on stumpy legs—Wilson was a capable center fielder.

"Wilson," said John McGraw, who managed Hack when he played for the Giants from 1923 through 1925, "is the greatest judge of fly balls I have seen since Tris Speaker."

Hack was also one of the great carousers in baseball history. Trying to curb Wilson's thirst for bootleg liquor, Cubs manager Joe McCarthy conducted a legendary experiment.

Marse Joe once placed two glasses on a clubhouse table. One filled with water, the other with Prohibition booze. He placed a worm in the glass of water, where it wriggled happily. McCarthy removed it, and then dropped it into the booze. The worm promptly died. McCarthy asked his players to draw a conclusion. Wilson spoke first.

"If you drink whiskey," Hack piped up, "you won't get worms."

In a 14-8 win over the Boston Braves on May 23, 1926, Wilson became the first player to hit a homer off the Wrigley Field scoreboard, then situated at ground level.

That night Hack was arrested for violating the Volstead Amendment while drinking beer at a friend's apartment.

Another time, Hack tried to duck the authorities during a raid but got stuck in a bathroom window.

B ill Veeck, who later owned the Cleveland Indians, St. Louis Browns, and Chicago White Sox, joined the Cubs front office in 1933. He recalled how Cubs trainer Andy Lotshaw tried to sober up Wilson before one contest.

Lotshaw placed Wilson in a big tub of water with a 50-pound cake of ice. Wilson kept trying to escape, and Lotshaw kept dunking the inebriated slugger's head into the frigid water.

"Every time Hack's head would bob up," mused Veeck, "Andy would shove it back down under the water and the cake of ice would come bobbing up. It was a fascinating site, watching them bob in perfect rhythm . . ."

According to Veeck, Wilson played that day and hit three homers in a single game for the first and only time in his career.

W ilson was the N.L. MVP for 1930, when he drove in 190 runs—a record that stood for the rest of the 1900s.

The 1931 season was a different story. Rogers Hornsby took over as Chicago manager in '31, and the N.L. introduced a new, less lively baseball. Complaining bitterly about the new ball, Hack slumped to .261 with 13 homers in 112 games.

T he no-nonsense Hornsby, meanwhile, wasn't happy with Wilson's extracurricular escapades. After benching Wilson in August, Hornsby inserted a pitcher in left field during one game while consigning Hack to the bullpen, where the disgruntled slugger warmed up pitchers.

After an altercation with sportswriters a few days later, the Cubs suspended Wilson for the remainder of the season.

Chicago unloaded Wilson after the '31 season. Three years later, he was gone from the majors. At various times, he tended bar, worked as a bouncer, freight-handler, and stevedore.

He was working as a laborer when he died in Baltimore at age 48. Wilson's body lay unclaimed until N.L. president Ford Frick paid for a coffin and his funeral.

When members of the Society for American Baseball Research reviewed Wilson's 1930 season, they discovered a discrepancy. Wilson, it turns out, had batted in one more run than the official records indicated, for a total of 191.

The SABRites passed along their findings to Major League Baseball. After a recommendation from MLB historian and longtime *Chicago Sun-Times* sports writer Jerome Holtzman, Wilson received credit for the extra RBI.

Wrigley Field

During the '50s, one of the most popular table games was Cadaco's All-Star Baseball. The game came with three-and-a-half inch discs that bore the names of major league stars. Printed on each disc's border were numbers that corresponded to hits or outs (1 = home run; 2 = ground ball; 3 = fly out; etc.).

Inside the game box was a flat-surface playing field and a stand-up scoreboard. On the flat surface were metal spinners, over which player discs were placed during an at-bat. After a spin, the tip of the spinner pointed to a number on the disc, determining the outcome of each play.

When assembled, the playing surface presented a beautiful sight—a vast expanse of green baseball field, confined by ivy-covered walls. An old-fashioned scoreboard sat atop the center field bleachers. The photograph was taken during an actual game, and the pitcher on the mound was just beginning his kick as the hitter in the batter's box was starting to coil. The view was from the press box.

Immediately below, behind short, red-brick walls, were the fans—so close to the action on the field, it looked like they could toss a bag of peanuts to the player in the visiting team's on-deck circle. The only thing missing was the smell of the hot dogs . . . and the wind.

The ballpark depicted was, of course, Wrigley Field. Cadaco All-Star Baseball came out when most telecasts were still in black and white. For a considerable number of post-World War II baseball fans growing outside Chicagoland, the game board provided the first chromatic view of a sports arena that does double duty as an *objet d'art.*

Yankee Stadium is majestic. Dodger Stadium is lavish. The home fields of the Mets and Phillies looks as if they were wrought by the same dull cookie cutter, and the Seattle Mariners' former home at the Kingdome was a monstrous birth.

Wrigley Field is as lovely an antiquity as the Parthenon, the Taj Mahal or the Baths of Caracalla. The Cubs' home field is art. Not graceful, serene and perfect, like a Raphaelite composition, but comfortable, charming and very American, like something out of Norman Rockwell.

Second only to Boston's Fenway Park in terms of longevity, Wrigley Field is a throwback to the days before America swallowed the hype; to a time when baseball was still a sport, and teams were as much a part of the neighborhood as the cop on the beat mom-and-pop grocery stores.

And the history! Restaurant chain owner Charles Weeghman built the park in 1914 for his team, the Chicago Whales of the Federal League. When the Feds folded after the 1915 season, Weeghman acquired the Cubs.

He moved them to Weeghman Field, as it was known, in time for the 1916 season. By 1927, the ball park was rechristened Wrigley Field, to honor the Cubs' new owners.

It was here that Hippo Vaughn of the Cubs and Cincinnati's Fred Toney hooked up in the famous "double-no hitter" of 1917. In 1932, Babe Ruth hit his final World Series homer in the Friendly Confines.

Wrigley Field was night baseball's last holdout. No night games took place there until August 9, 1988, when the Cubs beat the Mets, 6-4.

That inaugural night game had actually been post-poned for 46 years. The first major league night game was in 1935, and six years later the Cubs decided to add lights to Wrigley Field. Installation was to begin on December 8, 1941.

On December 7, the Japanese attacked Pearl Harbor and a day later the United States declared war on Japan. Owner Phil Wrigley scrapped the idea of adding lights to the ballpark, and donated the light towers to the Great Lakes Naval Air Station.

The Wrigley Field lights didn't make it back after the war. For the next 45 seasons, the Cubs continued to play all home games in daylight.

The scoreboard situated atop the center field bleachers was constructed in 1935 under the direction of Bill Veeck, at the time an up-and-coming Cubs' executive. The scoreboard is 27' high and 75' long. It is operated by hand. It wasn't until 1982 that any electronic device was installed in the scoreboard.

It was also Veeck who purchased the original vines of ivy for Wrigley's walls in 1937.

The flag that flies over the center field pole tells neighborhood fans how the Cubs have done in a game. A blue flag with a white 'W' indicates a victory, while a white flag with a blue 'L' signals a defeat.

Ernie Banks' uniform number, 14, is imprinted on the flag that flies from the left field foul pole. Over on the right field foul pole, a flag flies with Billy Williams' No. 26.

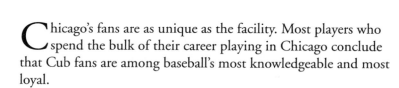

Chicago's fans are as unique as the facility. Most players who spend the bulk of their career playing in Chicago conclude that Cub fans are among baseball's most knowledgeable and most loyal.

Wrigley's denizens may also be the only fans for whom a play was written. *Bleacher Bums,* described as a "nine-inning comedy," was conceived by actor Joe Mantegna and written, in part, by Mantegna and Dennis Franz of *NYPD Blue* fame. *Bleacher Bums* takes place in Wrigley's right field bleachers during a 1977 game between the Cubs and Cardinals.

The characters are based on actual fans and incidents. Anyone who's sat in the bleacher seats during a Cubs home game will easily recognize Greg, Zig, Richie, Marvin, Cheerleader, Decker, and the others.

Cub rooters regenerate annually, as old fans pass on and young fans take their place. Baseball parks, however, only grow older. When vintage ballparks like Tiger Stadium are abandoned, baseball purists sadly shake their heads.

We pour concrete over a dirt path in the name of progress, they seem to say, and while it may be more efficient, we've lost something we'll never have again.

Somewhere in this favored land, there's got to be room for at least one unpaved country road. And true baseball fans everywhere hope—against all odds and logic, perhaps—that when another century dawns on Chicago, Wrigley Field will still be there on Addison Avenue, unchanged and beautiful as ever.

Zip Zabel

Talk about long relief! On June 17, 1917, the Cubs hosted Brooklyn at the West Side Grounds. With two outs in the first inning and the Dodgers up by a run, Zack Wheat buzzed a line drive that split a finger on the pitching hand of Chicago starter Bert Humphries.

Manager Roger Bresnahan had to put in an emergency call to right hander George Washington "Zip" Zabel.

All but forgotten today, Zabel pitched three seasons in the majors, all with the Cubs, from 1913 through 1915. But against the Dodgers on that late spring day in '15, Zabel set a big league record that may never be broken.

Zabel blanked the Dodgers until the eighth, when they tied the contest at two-all. He held them scoreless until the 15th, when Brooklyn eked out another run. But in the bottom of the frame, Vic Saier's homer into the right field bleachers kept the marathon going.

Finally, in the bottom of the 19th, Cubs shortstop Bobby Fisher scored the winning run from second base on a throwing error by Brooklyn second sacker George Cutshaw.

The final score was 4-3, and Zabel was the winning pitcher. Zip struck out six batters, gave up six hits and one intentional walk in the three-hour, 15-minute contest. But that day he earned a place—very likely permanent—in the record book.

His 18 and two-thirds innings were the longest relief job in major league history.

Bob Zick

By late July 1954 the Cubs were in the doldrums once again. The pitching was particularly atrocious, and for help the front office summoned Chicago native Bob Zick, a right-hander, from Beaumont of the Texas League.

According to legend, Zick dutifully reported to manager Stan Hack when he joined the team and introduced himself, saying, "I'm Zick."

"Oh, yeah?" deadpanned Hack, whose Cubs were en route to a sixth-place finish and a 72-82 record. "I don't feel so good myself."

Bibliography

Ahrens, Art, & Gold, Eddie. *The Complete Record of Chicago Cubs Baseball.* New York: Collier Books, 1986.

— *Day by Day in Chicago Cubs History.* West Point, NY: Leisure Press, 1982.

— *The Golden Era Cubs, 1876–1940.* Chicago: Bonus Books, 1985.

— *The New Era Cubs. 1941–1985.* Chicago: Bonus Books, 1985.

— *1985–1990: The Renewal Era Cubs.* Chicago: Bonus Books, 1990.

Alexander, Charles. *Rogers Hornsby: A Biography.* New York: Henry Holt & Co., 1995.

Allen, Lee. *The Hot Stove League.* New York: A.S. Barnes & Co., 1955.

— *The National League Story.* New York: Hill & Wang, 1961.

Allen, Lee, & Meany, Tom. *Kings of the Diamond.* New York: G.P. Putnam's Sons, 1965.

Anson, Adrian. *A Ball Player's Career.* Chicago: Era Publishing Co., 1900.

Aylesworth, Thomas, & Minks, Benton. In John S. Bowman, ed., *The Encyclopedia of Baseball Managers.* New York: Crescent Books, 1990.

Banks, Ernie, & Enright, Jim. *Mr. Cub.* Chicago: Follett Publishing Co., 1971.

Bartell, Dick, & Macht, Norman L. *Rowdy Richard.* Berkeley, CA: North Atlantic Books, 1987.

Bartlett, Arthur. *Baseball and Mr. Spalding.* New York: Farrar, Strauss & Young, Inc., 1951.

Benson, Michael. *Ballparks of North America.* Jefferson, NC: McFarland & Co., 1989.

Bjarkman, Peter C., ed. *Encyclopedia of Major League Baseball Team Histories: National League.* Westport, CT: Meckler Publishing, 1991.

— *Baseball With a Latin Beat.* Jefferson, NC: McFarland & Co., Inc., 1994.

Bosco, Joseph. *The Boys Who Would be Cubs.* New York: William Morrow & Co., Inc., 1990.

Boudreau, Lou, & Schneider, Russell. *Lou Boudreau: Covering All the Bases.* Champaign, IL: Sagamore Publishing, 1993.

Brickhouse, Jack. *Thanks for Listening!* South Bend, IN: Dia- mond Communications, 1986.

Brock, Lou, & Schulze, Franz. *Stealing is my Game.* Englewood Cliff, NJ: Prentice-Hall, Inc., 1976.

Bryan, Mike. *Baseball Lives.* New York: Pantheon Books, 1989.

Caray, Harry, & Verdi, Bob. *Holy Cow!* New York: Villard Books, 1989.

Cava, Pete. *The Encyclopedia of Indiana-Born Major League Baseball Players.* Work in progress.

Charlton, James. *The Baseball Chronology.* New York: Macmillan, 1991.

Coberly, Rich. *The No-Hit Hall of Fame: No-Hitters of the 20th Century.* Newport Beach, CA: Triple Play Publications, 1985.

Crissey, Harrington E., Jr. *Teenagers, Graybeards and 4-F's. Vol. I: The National League.* Trenton, NJ: White Eagle Printing Co., 1981.

Dawson, Andre, with Bird, Tom. *Hawk.* Grand Rapids, MI: Zondervan Publishing House, 1994.

Dewan, John, ed. *The Scouting Report: 1990.* New York: Harper& Row, 1990.

Durocher, Leo, & Linn, Ed. *Nice Guys Finish Last.* New York: Simon & Schuster, 1975.

Enright, Jim. *Baseball's Great Teams: The Chicago Cubs.* New York: Macmillan Publishing Co., 1975.

Erickson, Hal. *Baseball in the Movies: A Comprehensive Reference, 1915–1991.* Jefferson, NC: McFarland, 1992.

Fulk, David, & Riley, Dan. *The Cubs Reader.* Boston: Houghton Mifflin Company, 1991.

Fusselle, Warner. *Baseball . . . A Laughing Matter.* St. Louis: The Sporting News, 1987.

271

Gilbert, Bill. *They Also Served.* New York: Crown Publishers, Inc., 1992.

Gold, Eddie. "The Player They Called 'The Mad Russian'" *Baseball Digest,* September 1982, 67–70.

Goldstein, Richard. *Spartan Seasons.* New York: Macmillan Publishing Co., 1980.

Golenbock, Peter. *Wrigleyville: A Magical History Tour of the Chicago Cubs.* New York: St. Martin's Press, 1996.

Green, Paul. *Forgotten Fields.* Waupaca, WI: Parker Publications, 1984.

Greenberg, Hank, & Berkow, Ira. *The Story of My Life.* New York: Times Books, 1989

Greenwood, Chuck. "HOFer Williams Celebrating 29 Seasons at Wrigley Field." *Sports Collectors Digest,* October 29, 1999, 80–81.

Grimm, Charlie, & Prell, Ed. *Grimm's Baseball Tales.* Notre Dame, IN: Diamond Communications, 1983.

Herskowitz, Mickey. "When Lowrey K.O.'d Ron Reagan." *Baseball Digest,* August 1968, 58–60.

Hoffman, John C. *Hank Sauer.* New York: A.S. Barnes & Co., 1953.

Holtzman, Jerome, and George Vass. *The Chicago Cubs Encyclopedia.* Philadelphia: Temple University Press, 1997.

Honig, Donald. *Baseball When the Grass Was Real.* New York: Coward, McCann, & Geoghegan, Inc., 1975.

— *The Chicago Cubs: An Illustrated History.* New York: Prentice-Hall Press, 1991.

— *The Man in the Dugout.* Lincoln, NE: University of Nebraska Press, 1977.

Isaacson, Melissa. "Sammy Sosa: A Budding Star for White Sox." *Baseball Digest,* August 1990.

Kavanagh, Jack. *Ol' Pete: The Grover Cleveland Alexander Story.* South Bend, IN: Diamond Communications, Inc.,1996.

Kelley, Brent. *Baseball Stars of the 1950s: Interview with All-Stars of the Game's Golden Era.* Jefferson, NC: McFarland, 1993.

Kuenster, John. "Ryne Sandberg of the Cubs, Baseball Digest's 1984 Player of the Year." *Baseball Digest,* January 1985, 13–16.

Langford, Jim. *The Game is Never Over.* South Bend, IN: Icarus Press, 1980.

Levine, Peter. *A.G. Spalding and the Rise of Baseball.* New York: Oxford University Press, 1985.

Lieb, Frederick G. *The Story of the World Series.* New York: G.P. Putnam's Sons, 1949.

Marazzi, Rich, & Fiorito, Len. *Aaron to Zuverink: A Nostalgic Look at the Baseball Players of the Fifties.* Briarcliff Manor, NY: Stein & Day, 1982.

Marshall, William. *Baseball's Pivotal Era, 1945–1951.* Lexington, KY: University Press of Kentucky, 1999.

Mathewson, Christy. *Pitching in a Pinch.* New York: Putnam, 1912.

McGregor, Ed. "Mark Grace of the Cubs: A Non-Typical Cleanup Hitter." *Baseball Digest,* June 1990.

Mitchell, Fred. "Ryne Sandberg: He's Going to Get Even Better!" *Baseball Digest,* June 1984, 42–45.

Murdock, Eugene. *Baseball Between the Wars: Memories of the Game by the Men Who Played It.* Westport, CT: Meckler Publishing, 1992.

Nineteenth Century Baseball Stars. Kansas City, MO: The Society for American Baseball Research, 1989.

Obojski, Robert. *Baseball Bloopers & Other Curious Incidents.* New York: Sterling Publishing Co., 1989.

Pacini, Le. "Augue Galan Overcame Handicap to Star in Majors." *Baseball Digest,* February 1982, 73–76.

Peary, Danny, ed. *Cult Baseball Players.* New York: Fireside, 1990.

— *We Played the Game.* New York: Hyperion, 1994.

Phalen, Rick. *Our Chicago Cubs: Inside the History and the Mystery of Baseball's Favorite Franchise.* South Bend, IN: Diamond Communications, 1992.

Reichler, Joseph L. *The Great All-Time Baseball Record Book.* New York: Macmillan, 1981.

Reidenbaugh, Lowell. *Cooperstown: Where Baseball's Legends Live Forever.* St. Louis: The Sporting News Publishing Co., 1983.

Rust, Art. *"Get That Nigger Off the Field!"* New York: Delacorte Press, 1974.

Sandberg, Ryne, & Rozner, Barry. *Second to Home: Ryne Sandberg Opens Up.* Chicago: Bonus Books, 1995.

Santo, Ron, with Minkoff, Randy. *For Love of Ivy.* Chicago: Bonus Books, 1993.

Sargent, Jim. "Arm Injuries Limited Mayer to '15 Miunutes of Fame.'" *Sports Collectors Digest,* November 5, 1999, 120–121.

"Scouting Reports on 1958 National League Rookies." *Baseball Digest,* March 1958, 73.

Shatzkin, Mike, ed. *The Ballplayers.* New York: Arbor House, William Morrow, 1990.

Smith, Fred T. *Cub Tales & Trivia.* West Bloomfield, MI: Altwerger & Mandel Publishing Co., 1991.

Smith, Ira L., & Smith, H. Allen. *Low and Inside.* Garden City, NY: Doubleday, 1949.

Talley, Rick. "Bill Madlock Born to Hit." *Baseball Digest,* September 1975, 23–26.

Veeck, Bill, & Linn, Ed. *Veeck—As in Wreck.* New York: G.P. Putnam's Sons, 1962.

Voigt, David Q. *American Baseball.* 3 vols. University Park, PA: Pennsylvania State University Press, 1983.

Wasserstrom, Chuck. *1996 Chicago Cubs Information Guide.* Chicago: Chicago National League Ball Club, Inc., 1996.

Wheeler, Lonnie. *Bleachers: A Summer in Wrigley Field.* Chicago: Contemporary Books, 1988.

Wilbert, Warren, & Hageman, William. *Chicago Cubs: Seasons at the Summit.* Champaign, IL: Sagamore Publishing, 1997.

Williams, Billy, & Haag, Irv. *Billy: The Classic Hitter.* Chicago: Rand McNally & Co., 1974.

Newspapers consulted:
Baseball America
Baseball Weekly
Chicago Tribune
Indianapolis Star
New York Times
USA Today